Right from the Start

The basics of patchwork & quilting

Chris Franses
&
Barbara Chainey

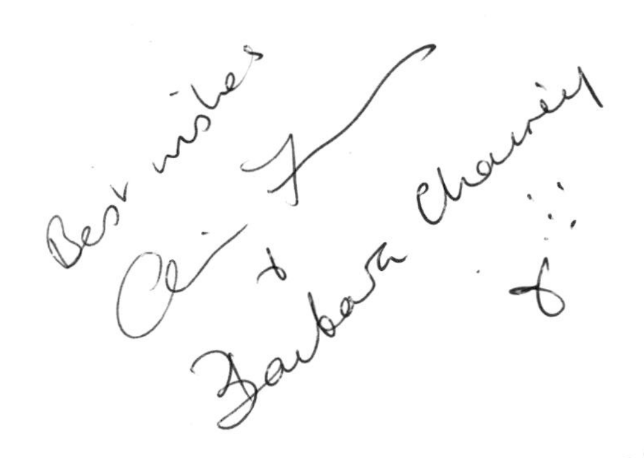

CRAFTWORLD SERIES

Published by Traplet Publications Limited 2010
Traplet House,
Pendragon Close,
Malvern,
Worcestershire. WR14 1GA
United Kingdom.

ISBN 978-1-900371-99-5

Printed by Wa Fai Graphic Arts Printing Co., Hong Kong

Contents

Acknowledgements

We'd like to thank Patchwork & Quilting editor Dianne Huck for timely pressure and encouragement. The design team at Traplet Publications have worked very hard to put this book in your hands, and we would both want to acknowledge the importance of our favourite quilt design program Electric Quilt. Thanks go also to our students, past and present, and various friends (you know who you all are) who, wittingly or otherwise, have helped along the way. Our long-suffering families have been tolerant of missed meals and general domestic chaos and we are now considering what our next plausible excuse for inactivity will be.

Introduction

and how to use this book

Right from the Start was originally conceived as an occasional series of basic "how to" articles for Patchwork and Quilting magazine. Almost immediately it became a regular series which generated a lot of very positive feedback, so much so that we thought it was worth collecting everything up into a book.

Beginning right at the start with equipment and finishing with binding, labels and hanging sleeves, you'll find information, step by step directions and tips to help you work through all the stages of making patchwork by hand or machine. We've included a project to try out your new skills – happy stitching!

Chris and Barbara

Equipment

What you need and how to use it

If you are just venturing into patchwork for the first time, the range of equipment you seem to need, or that is available for you to buy, seems terrifying. But, not all of it is absolutely necessary. If you enjoy hand sewing then you only need pins, needles and scissors, photo 1. If you want quick results then you will need to invest in a sewing machine and, probably, a rotary cutter, ruler and mat.

1. Hand sewing kit

The bare necessities

To make a patchwork quilt all you need is needle, thread, scissors and some fabric to cut up and sew back together again. But....

To make a really 'good' patchwork quilt you need a 'good' needle, 'good' cotton thread and cotton (dress weight) fabric. In addition, if you want to make more than one quilt in a lifetime, you will need a sewing machine and probably a rotary cutter, ruler and mat, photo 2.

2. Machine sewing kit

There are endless other things, wonderful sounding gadgets, to spend your hard-earned cash on, but the basics are a straightforward sewing machine, one rotary cutter, one mat and one ruler. Needles and thread you will need lots of, and different types, and as for fabric...... well, it goes without saying that you can never have too much.

Let's get the big expensive stuff out of the way first and work our way down to the smaller essentials. At the end of the chapter we will consider how to look after and use the rotary cutter.

Sewing machine

You will need a machine in good working order that will do an even, straight stitch, photo 3. And that's about it. However it will make life easier if your machine has one or two modern refinements. Speed control, especially if you are new to using a sewing machine, is a great invention as it can stop that awful feeling

3. Sewing machines

> **TIP**
>
> *If you are going to take your machine to classes, make sure it truly is portable – that you can lift it in and out of the car and carry it some distance.*

of not being in control as the machine runs away from you. The new foot controls will now advance the needle half a stitch at a time with a tap of the foot for super accuracy. A needle-down function keeps the needle down in the fabric when you stop sewing – again a huge advantage for accuracy. Most modern machines also come with an array of specialist feet designed for appliqué, piecing and quilting, such as the open-toed foot, free-motion foot, walking foot and ¼ inch foot.

Think about the sort of sewing you want to do and your budget; set your sights accordingly. Go to your local friendly sewing machine shop and chat to the man (it is invariably a man) in charge about the reliability of various makes and models that have taken your eye. Enquire about second-hand machines; they will usually have several in the shop from customers trading up to the latest all-singing, all-dancing model. Talk to people (including customers) in the quilting shops and at the quilting shows about their machines. Take the opportunity at quilt shows to go to the various manufacturers' stands and try out their machines, collect their brochures and then go back to your local shop armed with your new knowledge for another chat.

In the end, the machine you buy is down to your personal preferences and budget, but don't be swayed by the fact that a machine will do almost everything (except make the tea) when all you really need is a basic model.

Once you have your machine at home, learn how to use it. Read the handbook and find out how to change the feet, wind a bobbin, thread the needle (it sounds daft, but each make of machine is slightly different), whether you need to oil it, and how to replace the bulb. If you take your machine to classes take the handbook too, you may need it if your machine starts to play up and you can't guarantee that your tutor will know anything about your particular model. Above all, ensure you have it serviced regularly. If you do then it will reward you with many years of faithful service.

> **TIP**
>
> *If you plan on taking classes it's a good idea to label or identify all your tools in some way. You can write with biro on the wrong side of the mat, scratch your name with a compass point on the ruler, and use school name labels for cutters and scissors.*

Cutter, ruler and mat

These are the big three of the equipment world, right up there after the sewing machine in terms of frequency of use and need to have (photo 4). Buying these items in one splurge can be a good idea as there is often a package deal which will make it cheaper than buying them separately. How do you know which ones to buy? If you find a package deal from a reputable source like a quilt shop or at a quilt show we suggest you go ahead and make the investment and get using these important tools right away. We acquired our first sets a long time ago and have developed our own personal preferences over the years and we each use quite different brands of cutters and lengths of rulers. One thing we're agreed on however is size – we both think the 18in x 24in mat and the standard 45mm rotary cutter make a great start. Smaller mats and blades just make life difficult unless you know you're always going to be cutting one layer of fabric and one shape at a time.

4. Cutters rulers and mats

Scissors

You'll need a large-ish pair of scissors for cutting fabric, a second pair of scissors for cutting paper and a small pair of scissors for snipping threads. Label each pair clearly and keep them solely for your use – horror stories abound of finding best fabric scissors being purloined for DIY projects, trimming pasted wallpaper, cutting carpet. Check that all three pairs are comfortable for you to use before making the purchase and promise yourself that you will keep each pair well-sharpened.

Machine needles

Having spent a large sum of money on a sewing machine don't practise false economy by buying cheap needles – buy the best you can afford, preferably the ones recommended by the machine manufacturer. they will repay you several-fold as poor quality needles cause skipped stitches and frayed thread, not to mention frayed tempers.

Match the needle to the fabric – generally a size 11/75 is ideal for piecing; for quilting, as you will be sewing through more layers, a larger needle is better, usually a 14/90. Schmetz have even produced a needle specifically for quilting.

Equally, match the needle to the thread. If you are using a thick thread for quilting or decorative stitching you may find a 16/100 needle is better than a 14/90. For metallic threads, especially if you have problems with fraying, try a top-stitch needle as these tend to have a bigger eye.

Hand sewing needles

Start with a packet of sharps for piecing, appliqué and general stitching and a packet of betweens (sometimes billed as quilting) for quilting. It's a good idea to get the mixed packets of different sizes – usually sizes 5 to 10 – so that you can work out what size you prefer. Remember the bigger the number the shorter and finer the needle. Like everything else in life there is a difference between brands and everyone develops preferences. Start with what is easily available and go from there.

Thread

Again, there is a huge range of thread out there for you to choose from - so where do you start? We're going to assume that you'll be making your choices from cotton threads rather than polyester and general purpose "sewing" threads.

Colour issues first. If you are piecing by hand or machine you will drive yourself crazy if you try and match every fabric you use – we prefer to opt for the safe middle ground and use a dark neutral colour such as biscuit, or dove grey. We found that this works really well, so well in fact that we have sometimes used a dark neutral for quilting rather than trying to match thread to fabric. For hand and/or machine quilting a multi-shaded thread can be very effective.

Now let's consider the weight of thread to use. We both like to use quite a fine thread, a 50s or 60s count, for piecing either by hand or machine. It really can make a difference to the accuracy of your piecing as a fine thread "sits" down in the seam when it has been pressed whereas a thicker (say a 30s count) thread forms a slight ridge and takes up a little more room. Picky, picky, picky – but maybe it's a good habit to get into?!

And of course there is quality of thread. Look for a good quality cotton thread that is smooth along its length and is not furry or fuzzy – that cheap mega reel from the market is not such a good idea and will fill your machine with lint.

TIP

Change the needle often, whether you sew by hand or machine. Needles are the cheapest of all your tools and deserve to be used at their best.

TIP

Change your machine needle regularly – after about 8 hours sewing, or at the start of every project. Needles bend, burr and blunt easily any or all of which will give you a headache if you try to sew with them. If you hear a 'poc-poc' as you sew it's a sure sign the needle needs to be replaced.

Pins

Try short pins, long pins and medium pins, glass headed pins, flower headed pins. Make yourself a pincushion, fill it with wool or emery sand and use it. In our experience you can never have too many pins. Gone are the days when we put two large squares of fabric together and sewed a hopeful seam, now we pin all the time. The other pins you will eventually find a use for are safety pins. Not nappy pins, but quilting safety pins ideal for fastening the layers of your quilt together for machine quilting.

Templates

If you hand sew, or don't want to buy a rotary cutter and all its accessories, then you will need templates. You can buy these ready-made in acrylic or metal and also as pre-cut papers. You can of course make your own. For this you will need plastic – for durability, although card works well if you are only going to be cutting a few pieces. Template plastic, like most things, comes in a range of sizes and types which you can buy from most good quilt shops. It's easy to use, just trace the shape you require and cut out with scissors (but not your best fabric scissors please). The thrifty among us use old ice cream cartons, milk bottles and similar things for plastic templates and cereal packets for cardboard.

Fabric markers

Every week there is a new marker or so it seems. Which one should you buy? Which is the right one? There are so many! To begin with we recommend you find a cheap propelling pencil and one of those blue washout pens. These two markers will be a good start so long as you use them both with care. Pencil is great if you need to mark stitching or cutting lines on the wrong side of medium to light coloured fabrics and should always be used lightly. The blue washout marker is visible on a wide range of fabrics but take great care not to expose the marked lines to heat (iron, sunlight, radiator) or they will set permanently. Also take care to remove the lines correctly by immersing the work in cool or cold water without detergent. Our other favourite markers include water soluble crayons and those delightful rolling chalk wheels.

Daylight lamp/work lamp

What the interior designers are fond of referring to as "task lighting" is an important consideration for all your sewing. Whether you are choosing or cutting up fabric or stitching it back together again you'll find it really makes a difference to have a good worklight available in addition to general overhead lighting. We both have portable daylight lamps next to our sewing machines and cutting boards.

Irons and ironing board

These two important items of equipment are often overlooked, possibly because most households already have them. Remember that, as quilters, we press rather than iron so you are not taking on more ironing as such, rather you will be doing more pressing, which is a different thing entirely. So what you will need from an iron is a medium size, comfortable grip, steam facility and reasonable weight. These days irons are relatively inexpensive – you could have the luxury of one for your work only! Ironing boards come in a whole range of sizes and you don't need full domestic size. Look at some of the budget ranges in the big supermarkets – we've found some super fold up table top boards which are great for moving around the house and taking to class. One of our most-used ironing boards is made from two fabric boards covered with an old towel! Easy to transport, store, and easy on working space, this was an ingenious idea from US quilting legend Jean Ray Laury.

It does make your stitching life a whole lot easier if you can set an iron and ironing board up within hailing distance of your sewing machine. Many quilters swear by the aerobic benefits of having their pressing stations at some distance from their sewing machines and some have been known to separate the two with a flight of stairs for extra fitness (though I'm not convinced its working – Chris).

Books

Have you, like us, stood at quilt show book stands and recoiled in terror at the sheer number of books available? Overwhelmed by so much choice that you gave up and went in search of a reviving mug of tea instead? Life was much easier back in the dark ages when we started and there were only a couple of books available that weren't exclusively American. We would advise buying one general book to start off with. One that shows the basics of patchwork, appliqué and quilting in a format that suits you, whether it's through photos, diagrams or lots of words.

Once the basics are understood, then branch out and buy books to guide and inspire as you feel the need (and have the cash). Project based books can be good to practice techniques by following step-by-step instructions, and you don't have to use the same colours as in the book for your work. Design based books can provide you with hours of inspiration and bedtime reading while you mentally devise your masterpiece.

To summarise – buy what you can afford, when you feel you need it. It is perfectly possible to make beautiful quilts with a minimum of outlay.

Rotary Cutting

Now let's move on and look at how to use and care for the rotary cutter, ruler and mat. But if the thought of cutting fabric this way scares you, feel free to wander off to the Hand Piecing chapter where we explain about using templates and scissors to cut your fabric.

Rotary cutter

There are many types of rotary cutter on the market, and everyone has their favourite. If at all possible, try out a few first to see which one you find most comfortable to hold and use.

Self-healing cutting mat

This is essential and there are no substitutes. A word of warning: try to store your mat flat and away from heat or sun. Be especially careful if your workspace catches the sun – don't leave the mat out – it will buckle and warp permanently. The same applies if you leave it in the car. Mats can be quite brittle too, try not to drop them as they may chip.

Rulers

There are dozens of rulers on the market. The most useful is one about 6" x 24" with ½" and ¼" divisions marked and with 45°, 30°, and 60° lines. Treat your ruler gently and carefully, try not to drop it or fling it about, they are actually quite fragile. It is very easy to chip the edge of the ruler – if this happens you may need to buy a new one as the chip can blunt or nick your rotary cutter blade. Try to use the same ruler throughout a project – all rulers are not equal, and although the measurements may be only a tiny fraction of an inch out, those tiny fractions can add up over the large number of pieces in a quilt.

A few thoughts on safety

Rotary cutters are one of our favourite time-saving tools enabling us to cut pieces for a quilt in a fraction of the time taken using templates and scissors. However, as they are sharp enough to cut through up to eight layers of fabric at a time, they are also sharp enough to cut through carpets, kitchen tables and you. They should therefore be handled carefully and properly.

Before you use a rotary cutter become familiar with some essential dos and don’ts so that safety becomes habit.

DOs

- Use the rotary cutter with a self-healing mat.
- Keep the mat on a firm, steady surface; preferably at comfortable work-top height.
- Keep the safety cover on the blade except at the moment you are making the cut.
- Cut with the blade rolling away from your body.
- Change the blade when it becomes blunt, or nicked.
- Put the cutter away safely when you have finished using it – don’t leave it lying around for small children to find or husbands to borrow.

DON’Ts

- Never be tempted to use the rotary cutter to cut anything unless it is on the self-healing mat – don’t for instance try to snip threads or slice a length of ribbon whilst holding it.
- Never rest the mat on your knees, always place it on the table; or the floor if you must.
- Never, ever, ever put the cutter down without the safety cover in place; you could easily cover it with some fabric, forget its existence, scoop the fabric (and cutter) up in your hands and slice your fingers quite badly. And if you don’t, someone else will.
- Never cut towards or across yourself, always turn the fabric, or the mat and fabric so that you cut away from your body – the consequences of the blade slipping don’t bear thinking about.
- Never use the cutter for cutting anything but fabric. Save an old, used blade for cutting paper, card and template plastic.

Looking after your cutter

Look after your cutter and it will reward you with many years of faithful service. When you first get your cutter examine it carefully. Then take it apart noting how and where each washer and nut fitted – some people we know take digital photos of each stage, photos 5. Put each piece down in order

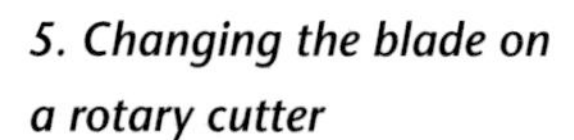

5. Changing the blade on a rotary cutter

a. Rotary cutter

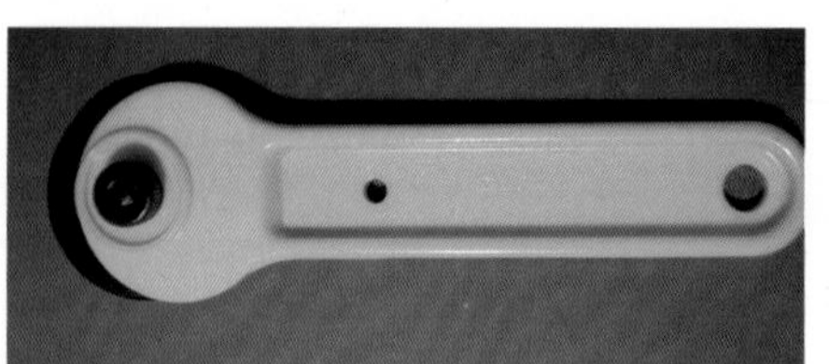

b. Rotary cutter back

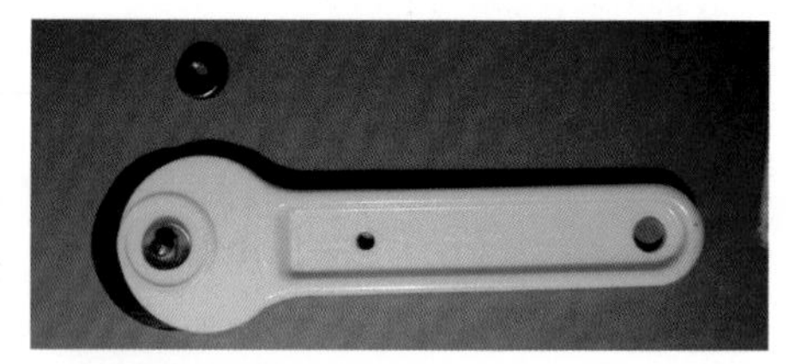

c. Remove nut

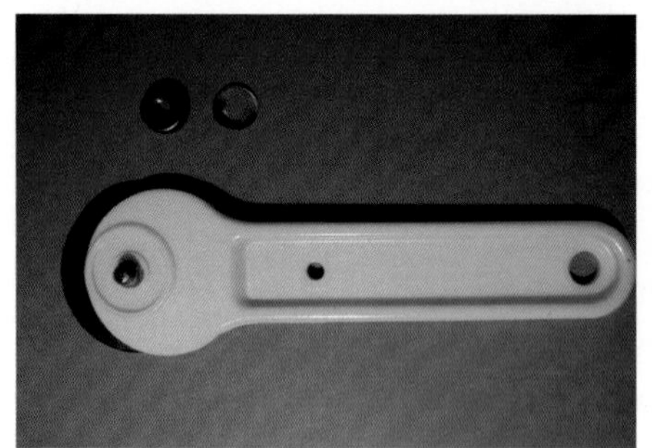

d. Remove washer

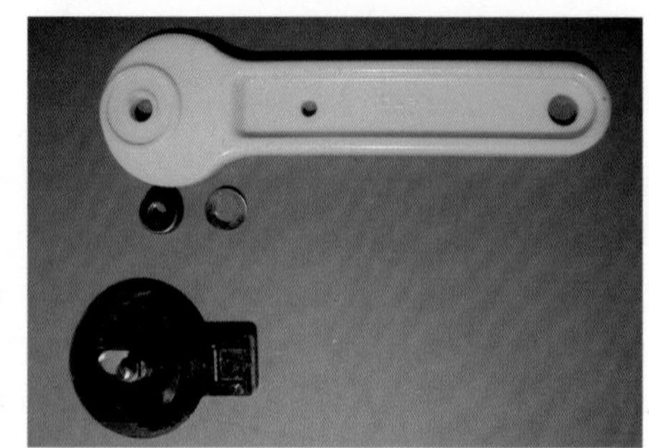

e. Remove handle

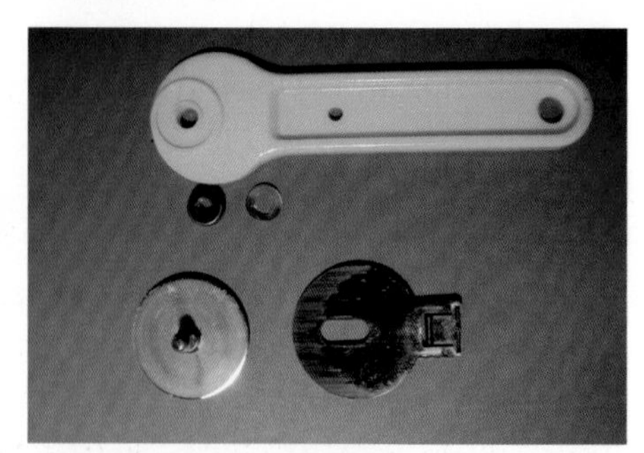

f. Remove blade guard

g. Replace blade, with care.

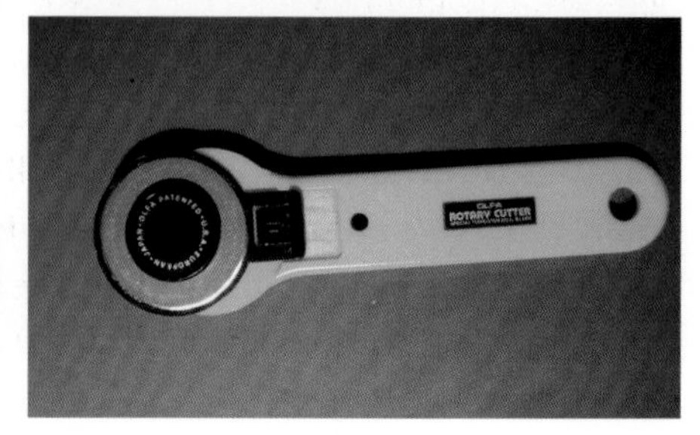

h. Cutter re-assembled

and in the position it came off – some washers, for instance, are curved so that they are more effective one way up than the other. Now, practice putting it back together again. After you have used the cutter a few times, take it apart and carefully wipe off the lint that has collected under the safety guard of the blade. You may also like to put a tiny drop of machine oil on the blade and wipe it – very carefully! Cut a few pieces of scrap fabric to get rid of any excess oil before using it on best fabric. Change the blade once it starts to become blunt or gets a nick in it. Blunt blades, like blunt knives, are more dangerous than sharp ones because of the extra effort involved in achieving a clean cut.

Cutting fabric strips – practice makes perfect

As with most things it takes a little practice to be able to use a rotary cutter efficiently and effectively. Stock up with some old sheets or fabric you hate and practice cutting these first before attempting to rotary cut your best fabric.

- Fold the fabric selvedge to selvedge, making sure it is hanging straight.
- Place it on the mat, lining up the fold at the bottom with a line near the bottom of the mat and the bulk of the fabric to your right (to your left if you are left-handed).
- Line the ruler up with a vertical line on the mat to cut the least amount of fabric necessary to straighten the edge. If you ensure the fold in the fabric is at right angles to the ruler and the line you cut, then you can be reasonably certain that you are cutting along the straight grain.

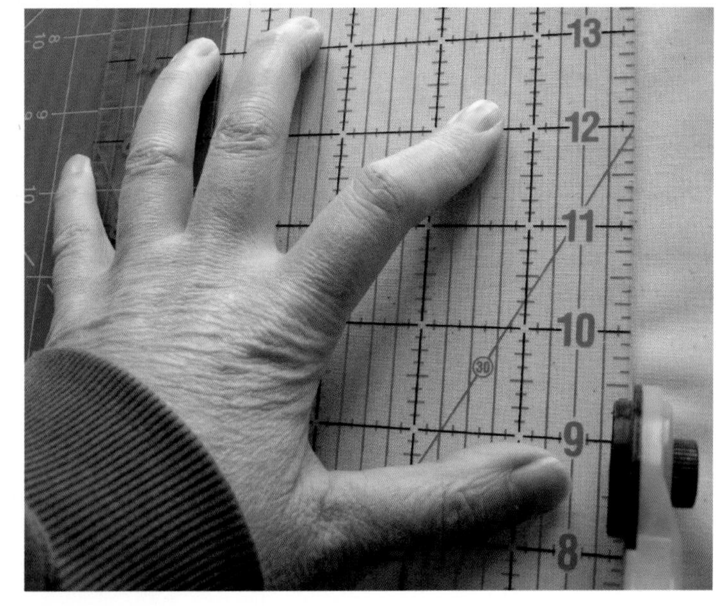

6. Hold the ruler steady

- Take the guard off the cutter, place the blade on the mat near the folded edge of the fabric (not on the fabric itself), flat against the edge of the ruler and hold it at about 45° to the mat.
- Hold the ruler in place with your left hand (right if left-handed), keeping your fingers out of the way, photo 6, and with a firm and even pressure roll the blade along the ruler through the fabric. Don't be afraid to stop part way through the cut, but don't lift the cutter. You will need to 'walk' your hand up the ruler to keep it steady as you cut against it and to start with you will feel better if you stop cutting when you move your hand. You must hold the ruler firm and still otherwise your cut will be a wobbly line instead of the nice straight one you were anticipating. Try placing your little finger on the worktop against the ruler as a little assistance to holding it firm. If the fabric was too long for the mat, stop cutting when you reach the edge of the mat and put the guard back on the cutter. Carefully slide the remaining fabric onto the mat. Line the ruler up with the cut you have just made and continue cutting.
- When you reach the end put the guard back on the cutter. This first cut is very important as it straightens the fabric and ensures that all subsequent cuts will be on the straight grain.
- Fold your fabric carefully in half again, lining up the newly cut raw edges. If the fabric is very wide you may wish to fold it a second time. Again keep the bulk of the fabric to your right (left if you are left-handed). You should now have a much shorter length of fabric to cut, which makes life a little easier.

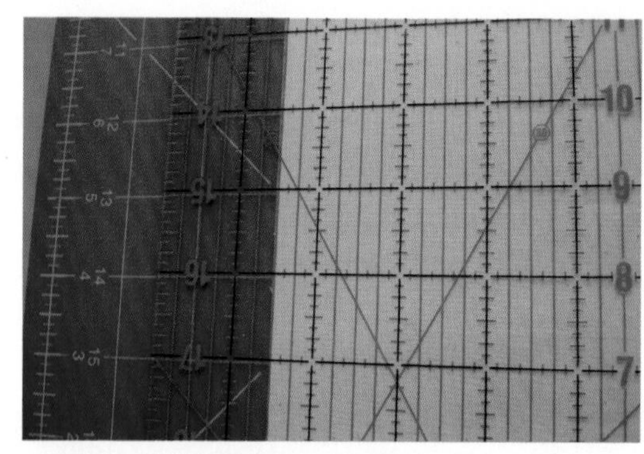
7. Align the ruler before cutting

• Check the width of strip you wish to cut and find this measurement on the ruler. Place the ruler on the fabric so this measurement is lined up with the cut raw edge, photo. 7. You may want to mark this measurement on the ruler if you are making more than one cut – a piece of tape is ideal. Remember – measure twice, cut once!
• Take the guard off the cutter, place the blade of the cutter on the mat against the ruler as before and with a firm, even pressure roll the cutter away from you through the fabric till you reach the mat at the other end. If you haven't cut through all the layers just try again. You may need to exert quite a lot of pressure on the cutter to cut through the layers so don't be afraid to press hard. After a bit of practice you can judge how hard to press down and cutting suddenly seems much easier. The trick is to have confidence in your ability to do it, then you will be surprised by how easy it is; but if you have convinced yourself it will be difficult, then it will be.
• Open out the strip you have cut and check that it is straight. If it has a kink in it then the first cut to straighten the fabric must have wandered.
• Either, open out the fabric and start again by folding it selvedge to selvedge and repeat the cut to straighten the edge. Or, if it is straight, then carry on cutting strips. Check every three or four strips to make sure they are straight. It is good practice to open out the fabric and straighten the edge again every 3 to 4 cuts in any case.

Once you feel confident cutting your old sheet into strips, try cutting some shapes from these strips.

Squares
These are relatively easy to cut. If, for instance, we want to cut 4" finished size squares, then first cut a strip ½" wider than your finished square (this is your ¼" all round seam allowance) i.e.4½".
• Without unfolding the strip, place the ruler across the strip, lining up the long raw edge with a straight line on the ruler and neaten the ragged short end of the strip.
• Now place the ruler across the strip again, lining up a straight line on the ruler with the long raw edge of the strip, and the measurement you want to cut your square (4½") with the short raw edge, which you have just neatened, photo. 8.

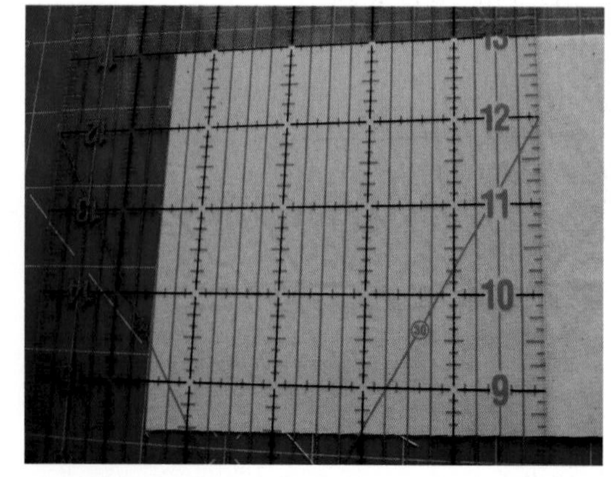
8. Cutting squares

• Cut along the edge of the ruler and you will have cut a square. If you haven't unfolded your strip you will, of course, cut four to eight squares at a time; which is what rotary cutting is all about.

Rectangles
These are cut in exactly the same way – cut a strip the width of the rectangle plus two times the seam allowance – ½" – and slice off rectangles to the required size; not forgetting to add that vital ½" seam allowance. In other words, if we want to cut rectangles that finish at 4" x 2" we could cut a 4½" strip as before and slice it into 2½" segments. Or cut a 2½" strip and slice it into 4½" segments.

Basic strips, squares, and rectangles can be sub-cut into triangles, diamonds or any shape you need – with the aid of the rotary cutter, the ruler, and (sometimes) a little tape.

Half-square triangles

Made by cutting a square in half diagonally, dia. 1 and photo 9.

- Add ⅞" seam allowance to finished size required.
- So if we wanted 4" finished squares again, cut a 4⅞" strip, and cut it into 4⅞" squares. Then cut in half diagonally, using the 45° line on your ruler or mat as a guide.

These half-square triangles are used in blocks such as Friendship Star, dia. 1c, Shoo Fly, dia. 1d, Maple Leaf, dia. 1e, and Pinwheel, dia. 1f.

9. Cutting half-square triangles

dia. 1 Half-square triangles

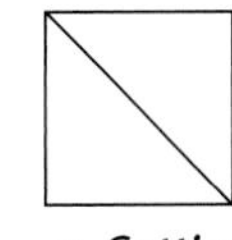
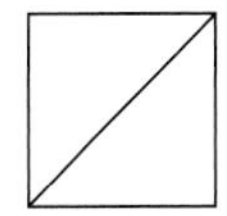

a. Cutting triangles

b. Friendship Star ***c. Shoo Fly***

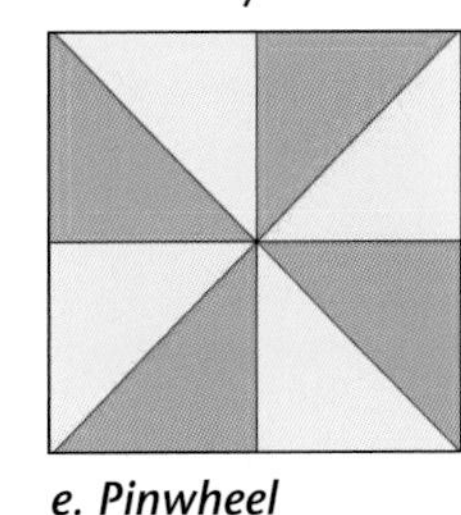

d. Maple Leaf ***e. Pinwheel***

Quarter-square triangles

These are made by cutting a square in four across the diagonals, dia. 2a and photos 10.

- Add 1¼" seam allowance to the finished size required.
- So if we wanted a 4" finished square, we would cut a 5¼" strip and cut this into 5¼" squares, then cut the squares into triangles.

These are used in blocks such as Big Dipper, dia. 2b, and Ohio Star, dia. 2c.

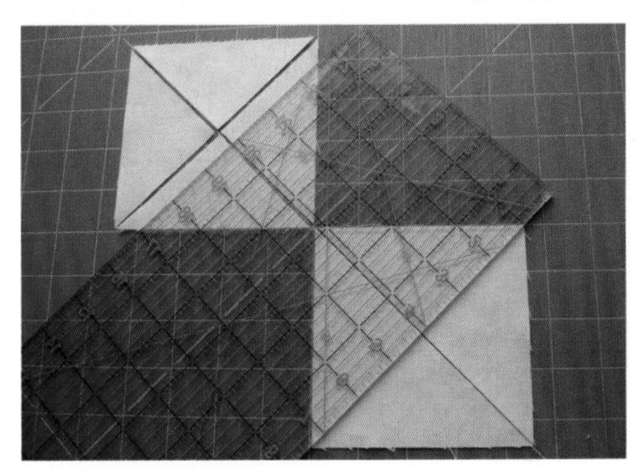

10. Cutting quarter-square triangles

dia. 2 Quarter-square triangles

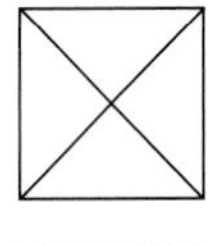

a. Cutting triangles

b. Big Dipper

c. Ohio Star

Half-rectangles

These triangles are made by cutting a rectangle in half along the diagonal.

- Add 1¼" seam allowance to the length and ⅝" to the width of the size required.
- So, once more using a 4" x 2" finished size as an example, we would cut a 5¼" x 2⅝" rectangle. Take care to cut the diagonal the right way, dia. 3a, otherwise you end up with a mirror image of your shape.

These are found in blocks such as Pinwheel Square, dia. 3b and 54-40 or Fight, dia. 3c.

dia. 3 Half-rectangles

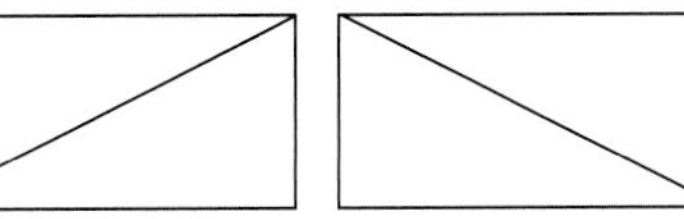
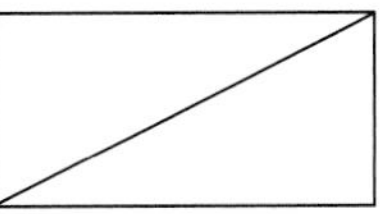

a. Cutting rectangles

b. Pinwheel Square

c. 54-50 or Fight

Using the angle lines

To cut these shapes use the angle lines on your ruler, or mark the correct angles with a length of masking tape. You may find it easier to outline the whole shape on your ruler with tape. Don't leave the tape on for too long or it will not peel off easily and will leave a residue. There is now a new non-sticky tape available in fetching neon colours which does a great job of highlighting the selected line/measurement on the ruler.

60° triangle

Cut a strip ¾" wider than the required height of the triangle and add ⅞" to the finished length. Line the 60° line on the ruler up with the long edge of the strip to make the first cut, photo 11 - 12. Turn the ruler over and line up the 60° line with the cut edge, photo 13 - 14. So, our 4" finished size will be cut from a 4¾" wide strip and the triangles cut at 4⅞" intervals.

These are used in 'pyramid' quilts. Six put together will make a hexagon.

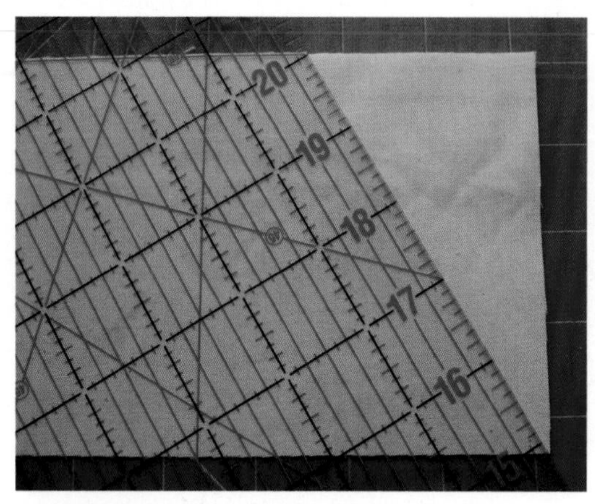

11. Using 60° line on the ruler

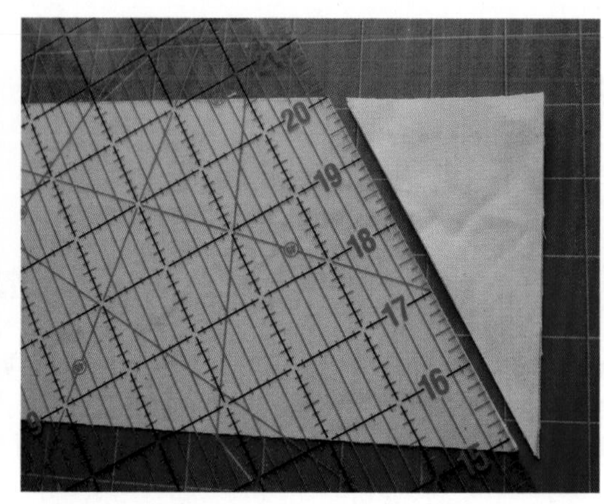

12. First 60° cut made

13. Cutting 60° triangle

14. 60° triangle

Diamonds

30° Cut a strip ½" wider than height of diamond, Add 1" to finished length. These are used very occasionally.

45° Cut a strip ½" wider than height of diamond. Add ¾" to finished length.

These are used in 8-pointed Star designs, dia. 4.

dia. 4.
8-pointed Star

60° Cut a strip ½" wider than the height of diamond, add ⅝" to finished length.
Again, use the 60° line on the ruler, photo 15 - 17. Mark the cutting line with a piece of tape as before, if necessary.

These are used in designs such as Tumbling Blocks or Storm at Sea, dia. 5.

15. Cutting 60° diamond

16. Cut made

17. Diamond cut

dia. 5.
Storm at Sea

Using colour and choosing fabrics

"But I'm no good with colour!" "Colour" is not outrageously technical or difficult. It is something which influences us all in our everyday lives - what we're all really seeking is some colour **confidence** to reassure us when we're picking out the fabrics for our next quilting project. Whatever colour and fabric choices you make we strongly recommend that you buy fabric you like and then (deep breath) use it. If you cut fabric up and use it you get twice the enjoyment from it. Consign it to your stash and it may stay there forever or at least long enough so that it finally looks dated and unappealing – ask us how we know this!

Here's an easy strategy to start you off. First, choose your favourite colour. Let's say it's blue. Find a pale blue, a bright blue, and a dark blue. Teaming these three **values** of one colour in the same project will give you a light, a medium and a dark which you could use for background, main and accent choices. But of course everything will be blue! Introduce variety (which as we all know is the proverbial spice of life) by changing the background or light blue for a pale pink or a pale yellow – in other words, keeping the same value but switching to a contrasting warm colour. See how the **contrast** between the **warm** and **cool** colours makes the selection livelier. We've used one of our favourite traditional blocks, Ohio Star, to show some of the many possibilities you could explore, dia. 1.

Still using the Ohio Star block as our example but this time putting it into a basic quilt setting shows how it can be much more interesting to use variations of placement and colour rather than just repeating the same block, dia. 2.

dia. 1
Ohio Star examples

a. Ohio Star 3 values of blue

b. Ohio Star same values of blue, change background to pale yellow

c. Ohio Star same values of blue, change background to pale pink

d. Ohio Star same values of blue, change centre triangles to mid yellow

e. Ohio Star same values of blue, change centre triangles to mid pink

f. Ohio Star same values of blue, change background to pale yellow and centre triangles to mid pink

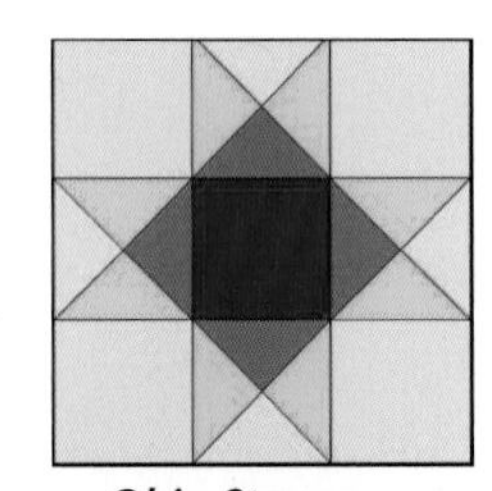

g. Ohio Star same values of blue, change main star points to dark yellow

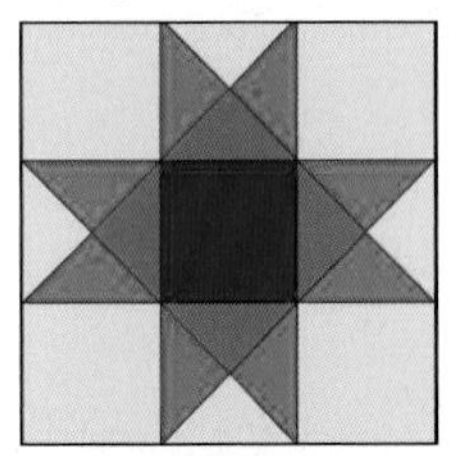

h. Ohio Star same values of blue, change main star points to dark pink

dia. 2
Ohio Star quilt settings

a. 9 block Ohio Star quilt 3 values of blue

b. 9 block Ohio Star quilt same values of blue change background to pale yellow and centre triangles to mid pink

c. 9 block Ohio Star quilt using 5 blocks one colouring and 4 blocks alternative colouring

d. 9 block Ohio Star quilt using 4 blocks one colouring, 4 blocks alternative colouring and 1 centre block in third colouring

e. 9 block Ohio Star quilt coloured as one larger block

dia. 3 Ohio Star blocks showing use of complementary colours

a. Ohio star block orange, violet, green

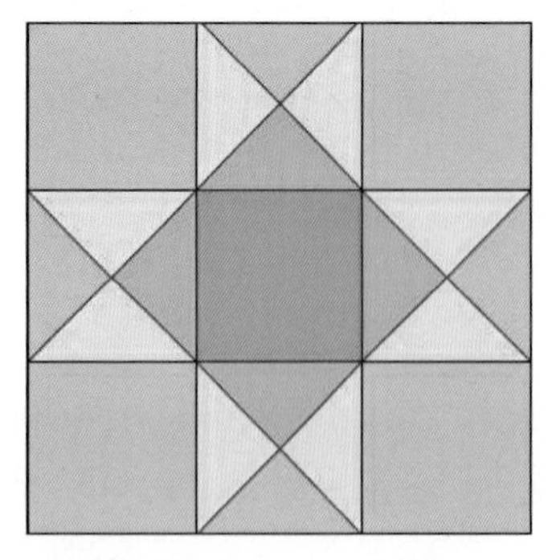

b. Ohio star block variation orange violet green

c. Ohio star block variation orange violet green

Including one or more **complementary** (opposite) colour can really perk up a colour scheme. For example orange and violet are complementary colours for green – not a combination that comes readily to mind perhaps but you can see from the examples that it is not an impossible mix, dia. 3.

One of our best buys was a small colour wheel – you'll find them at art shops or good quilt shops – which has a pointer reference system. Now we can easily find complementary colours to use with our main choices and make our colour schemes more interesting. We also visited our local DIY shop and collected up a full set of those wonderful paint shade cards and had lots of fun cutting them up and making artistic colour compositions! This is a great way to play with colour and try things out without harming your precious fabric stash. Look through magazines and books for pictures that you find appealing or striking. You can get plenty of colour scheme inspiration this way and most of the work is already done for you. Really look at the colours in each picture and pick out equivalents from the paint cards – have fun!

And if you're aiming to perk things up without too much effort it is always worth considering the addition of a judicious dash of **drama** to your original selection. Just switching your background value from light to dark can make a huge difference, dia. 4.

dia. 4
Effects of changing background colour

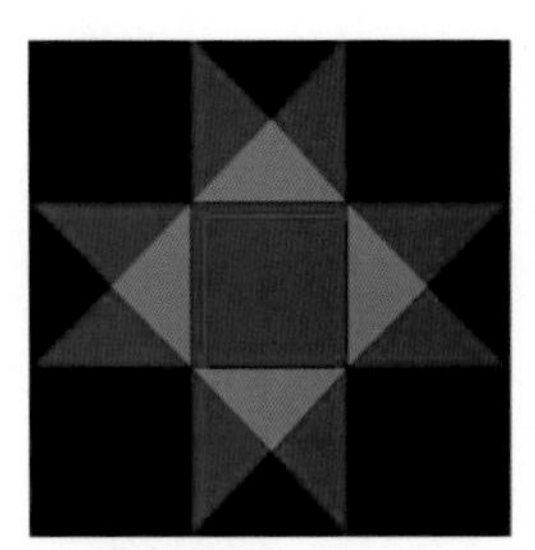

a. Ohio star block original 3 values of blue, change background to black

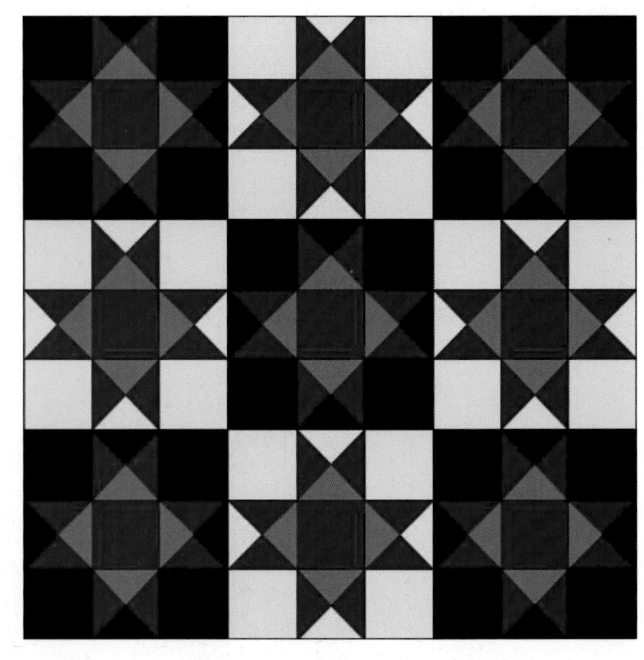

b. 9 block Ohio star quilt alternating these 2 blocks

1. Five basic colours taken from the main print

2. The effect of adding a bright to the basic palette

3. Adding a third light mauve

So far we have been looking at examples with only solid colours – what happens when you're confronted with all those yummy fabrics out there in the quilt shops and you're dealing with not only colour but print as well? Just how do you choose printed fabrics and make them work for you?

A really easy route to colour confidence is to pick out the colours from a main print and use them in a similar ratio, photos 1 - 3. If you have a selvedge strip from the main print you may have the colour tabs printed out to make your matching even easier, photo 4.

If all your choices are of a similar scale and value you will achieve a blended look where shapes merge into each other and only the **colours** lead the eye, photo 5. This works well for quilts using a single large shape such as squares or diamonds. You'll find fabulous examples of this approach in Kaffe Fassett's work.

4. Selvedge edge showing colours

5. Similar fabrics blend and merge

You've decided on a main colour scheme or theme – let's be daring and take turquoise/jade rather than basic blue in our next Ohio Star examples to show some of the effects of **scale** and **value** in printed fabrics.

dia. 5
Using prints in Ohio Star blocks

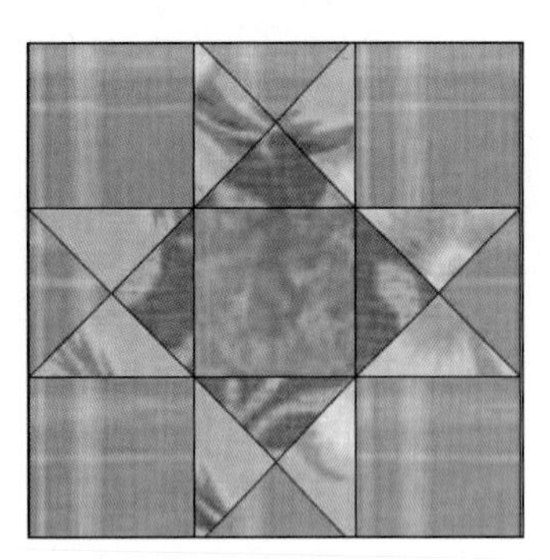

a. Fabrics of similar value

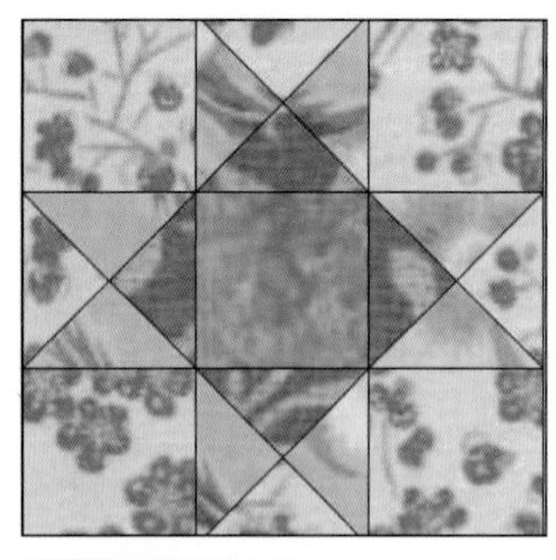

b. Change background colour but not scale

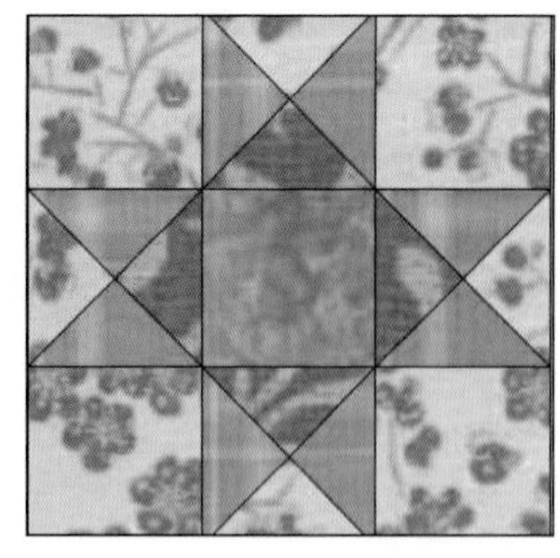

c. Change star point fabric

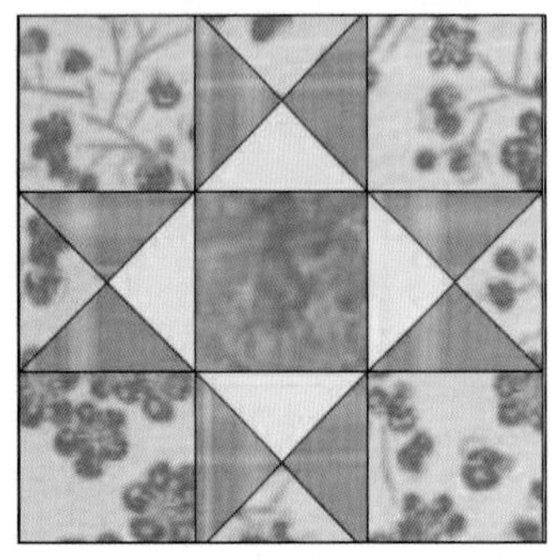

d. Change centre colour

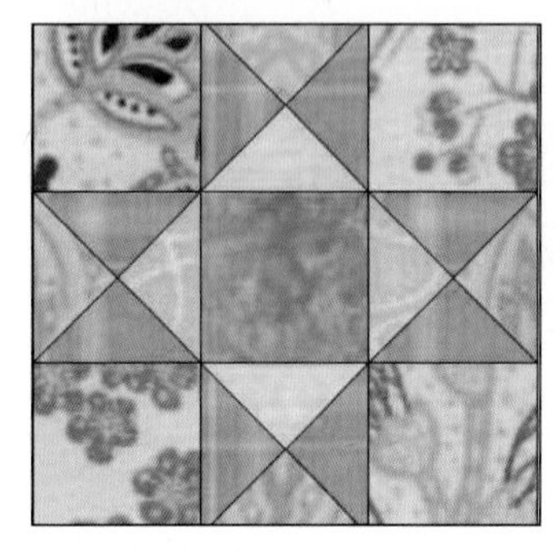

e. Using more fabrics

Our first Ohio Star block, dia. 5a, shows four fabrics of similar value. Three are turquoise, one is a complementary warm buff. The three turquoise fabrics are similar in scale, the buff fabric is a smaller scale print.

Changing the background fabric in colour but not scale of print is what we see in dia. 5b – the four corner squares and main star points still appear blended but the centre square now "pops" right out.

In dia. 5c we have changed the large scale floral star points to the turquoise plaid and straightaway the star is clearer. The scale of the print remains the same but there is a contrast between the straight lines of the plaid and the lines of the background print. There is also more colour contrast (complementary) between these two fabrics.

In dia, 5d we lighten and brighten the block at the centre by changing the neat buff print to a sharp yellow.

Dia. 5e takes things much further on down a multi-fabric path – now we have two different prints for each of the main "positions" in the block making a total of eight fabrics. Look how far this is from the very first Ohio Star example we gave.

You can achieve clarity and definition with your fabric choices by including a variety of scale – perhaps taking a large scale multi colour print as the starting point and adding in both medium and small scale prints in different values and colours, photos 6 - 8. Look for different **textures** in the prints – stripes, checks, spots – to add further interest and contrast to your selection, even when using only one colour as Margery Blundy has in her Blue Ohio quilt, photo 9.

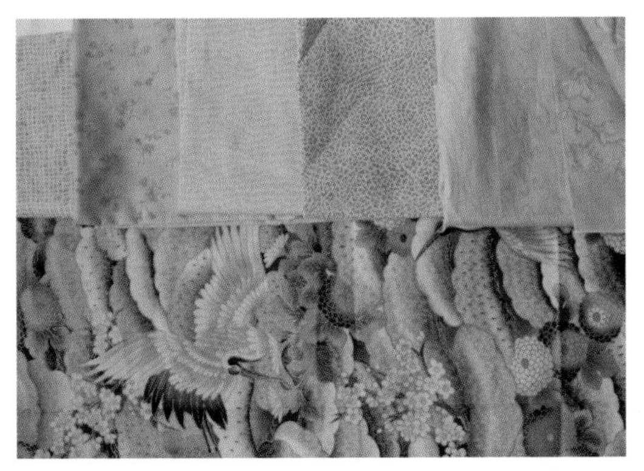

6 Adding prints of different scale and value

7. Adding prints of different colours and scale

8. Adding prints of different colour, scale, and value

9. Margery's Blue Ohio quilt

For colour play we used paint shade cards, for fabric play try old swatch cards from fabric shops, or sample squares from mail-order quilt shops. For playing with big prints and big scale try asking at your local interior decorators for unwanted wallpaper books, these are brilliant for cutting up to try out ideas of colour and scale.

Fabric

Use dress-weight cotton whenever possible. Other fabrics can be, and are, used in patchwork and appliqué but the best results are achieved with cotton especially when you first start. It will crease and hold its shape much better than man-made fibres. It is also best to stick with similar weights and types of fabrics in the same piece of work.

Should you pre-wash your fabric? It depends! If it is a deep dark colour and you are making something which will be washed then it might be an idea to test it for colour fastness before you use it. If it runs, then, yes, wash it – perhaps with something to help fix the dye if it keeps running. If you can't stop it running then perhaps you should consider using a different fabric, or make sure you use a 'colour catcher' when you wash the quilt. Otherwise, it's up to you. There are two schools of thought – washing removes the 'finishing' on the fabric – this can make it easier to handle, equally it can make it more prone to stretch (which is where starch comes in handy). Neither of us pre-wash our fabrics – but then we're also bone idle! Many quilters we know do wash their fabrics and derive great pleasure from pressing and folding newly washed purchases and storing them away in a project box.

Patchwork blocks

Basic units of patchwork

It may seem odd to devote an entire chapter to 'blocks' but patchwork is stitched from geometric shapes. If you look closely, even the most complex of quilts can usually be broken down into smaller units of blocks (which can be broken down again into even smaller units) or repeating single shapes such as hexagons, squares, diamonds, triangles, and rectangles, dia. 1. Single shape quilts are often referred to as 1-patch quilts.

dia. 1. 1-patch quilts

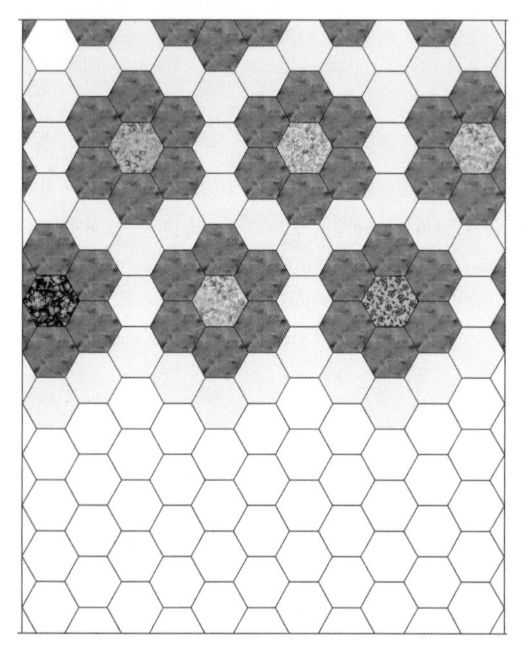

a. Hexagons – Grandmother's Flower garden

b. Squares – Trip around the World

c. Rectangles – Rail Fence

d. Triangles – Pyramids

Blocks are usually categorised by a basic grid, or the number of units they contain – so a 4-patch block will have a basic grid of 4 units, dia. 2, a 9-patch block will have a grid of 9 units, dia. 3; this system extends to 4x4 grids, dia. 4, 5x5 grids, dia. 5.

dia. 2. 4-patch blocks (2 x 2 grid)

dia. 3. 9-patch blocks

dia. 4. 4-patch blocks (4 x 4 grid)

dia. 5. 5-patch blocks (5 x 5 grid)

Units within a block can be subdivided, usually with straight lines, in a variety of different ways: into rectangles or squares, dia. 6, or triangles, dia.7, or irregular shapes, dia. 8.

dia. 6. Rectangles and squares

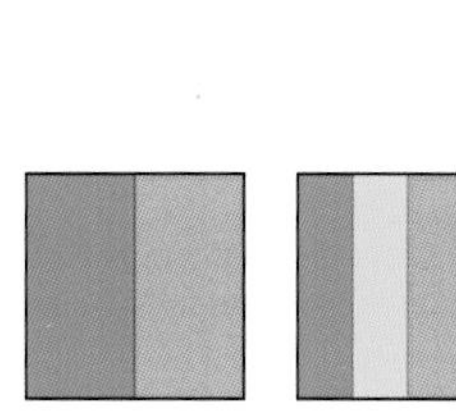
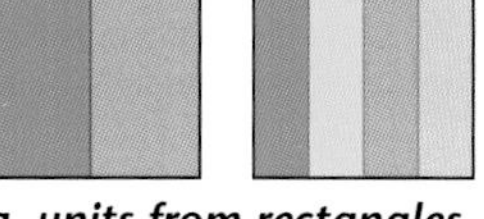

a. units from rectangles

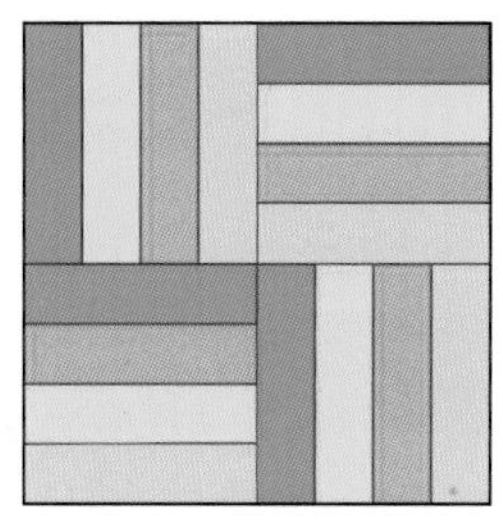

b. Railfence block

c. units from squares

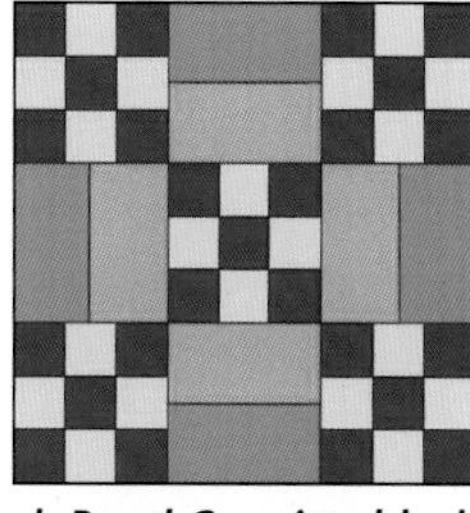

d. Road Crossing block

dia. 7. Triangles

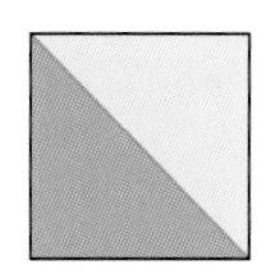

a. Half-square triangle

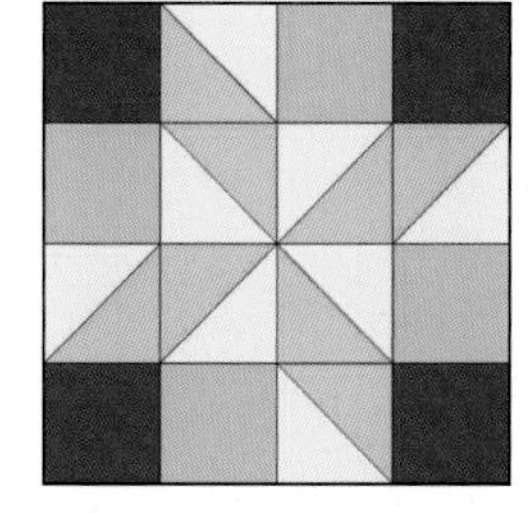

b. Clay's Choice block

c. Quarter-square triangle

d. Ohio Star block

e. Isosceles triangle

f. 54-40 or Fight block

g. 3-triangle unit

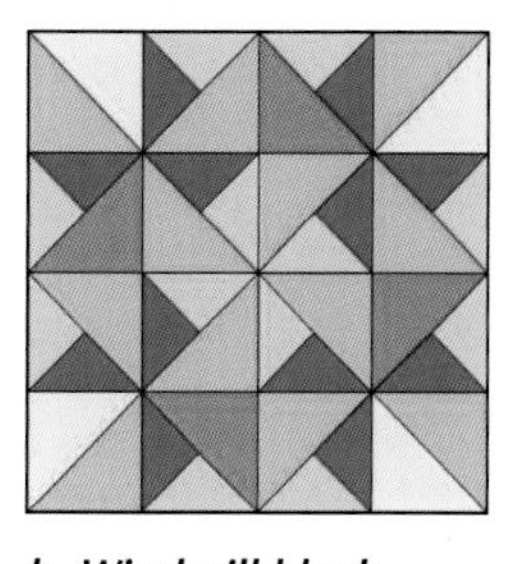

h. Windmill block

dia. 8. Irregular shapes

You can have a lot of fun playing with divisions within a square unit and then grouping units into blocks of your own. Start with a pencil, a few crayons or felt tip pens and some squared paper and see what you come up with. Try a 4-patch grid first, then a 9-patch and just have fun making divisions and colouring in shapes. Remember, the arrangement of units in a block does not necessarily have to follow tradition and be symmetrical, dia. 9. Four non-symmetrical blocks grouped together may lead you on to a larger (and symmetrical) block, dia. 10.

dia. 9. Symmetry

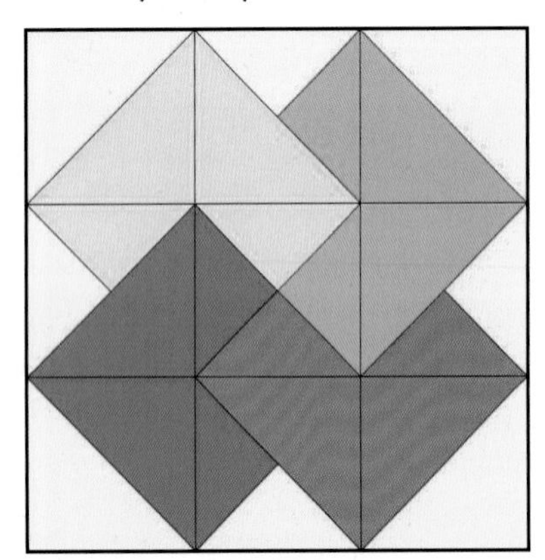

a. A symmetrical block (Card Trick)

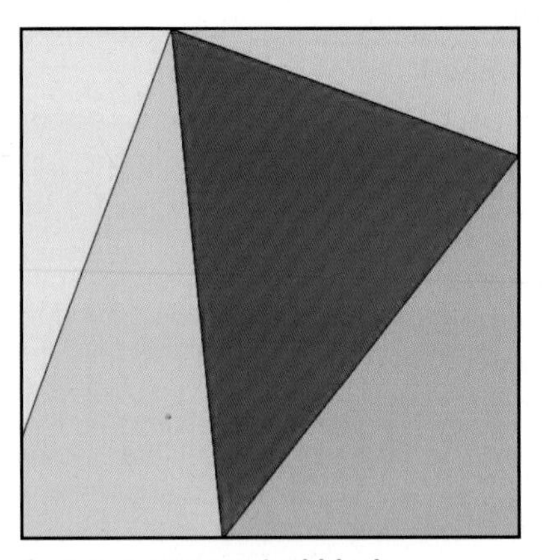

b. A non-symmetrical block

dia. 10. 4 Creating larger blocks

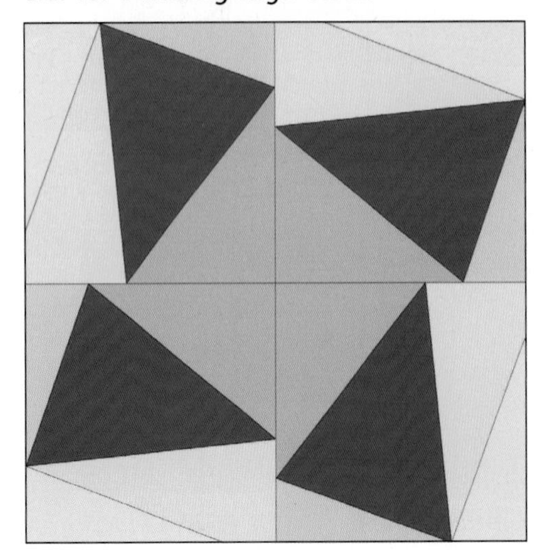

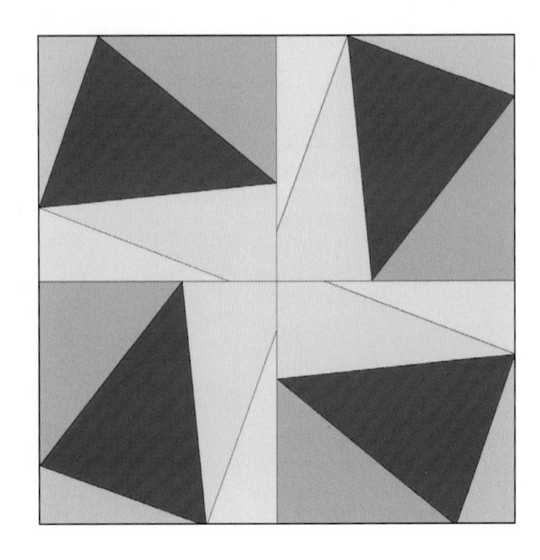

The more technically-minded of you may prefer to use a computer rather than pencil and paper. You can draw designs in 'Word' or in 'Paint', both of which come ready-loaded on most PCs. Or, you can go really technical and buy a quilt design program for your computer. The two best known are probably Electric Quilt (EQ) and Quilt-Pro. Look on their websites for information about them and stop off at one of the big quilt shows to see them being demonstrated. Electric Quilt allows you to draw block designs using lines (as you would use a pencil) whereas Quilt-Pro allows you to design blocks by first making 'patches' and then putting these together (as you would if making a block from fabric). They both have excellent libraries of pre-drawn blocks and fabric so you can design a quilt and they both have the facility to calculate how much fabric you need to buy for that quilt.

As we said earlier, quite complex quilts can be broken down into a series of smaller units. Have a look at this design, dia. 11. It looks very intricate, but is actually made from squares and triangles carefully coloured to give an overall design.

dia. 11. Find the units

All the designs we've looked at so far are made from straight lines, but you can use curved lines too, dia.12. The next trick is to use straight lines to give the illusion of curves. Using different shapes of triangle is usually the best way to achieve this, dia.13.

dia. 12 Curved seam blocks

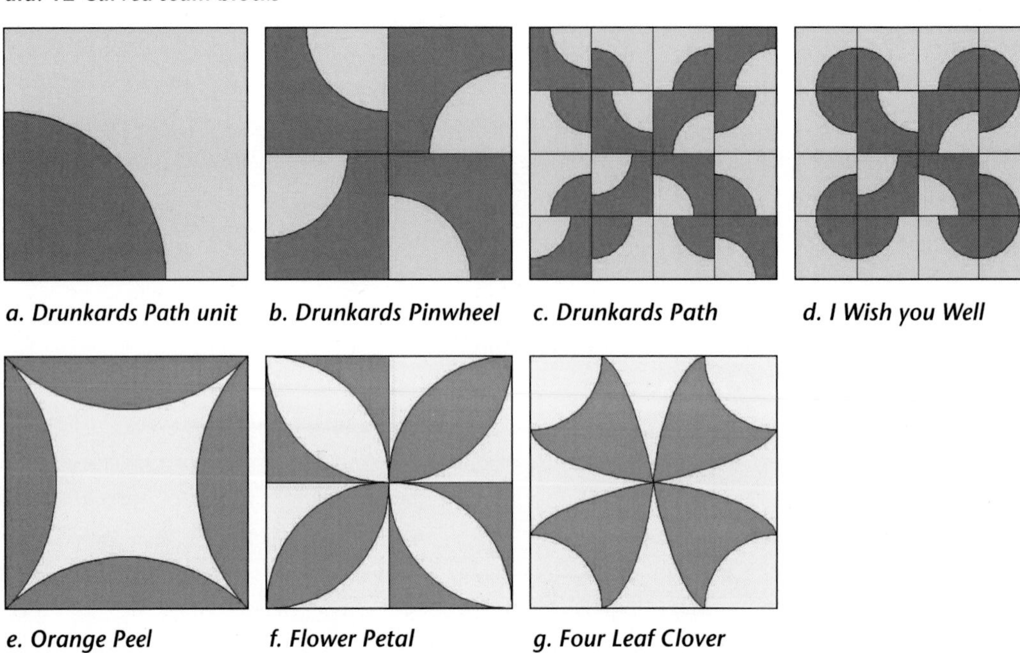

a. Drunkards Path unit ***b. Drunkards Pinwheel*** ***c. Drunkards Path*** ***d. I Wish you Well***

e. Orange Peel ***f. Flower Petal*** ***g. Four Leaf Clover***

dia.13. Illusions of curves

a. Storm at Sea block

b. Storm at Sea quilt

TIP

Don't draw anything you might find too complicated to make; unless, of course, you have no intention of ever making it!

c. Star variation

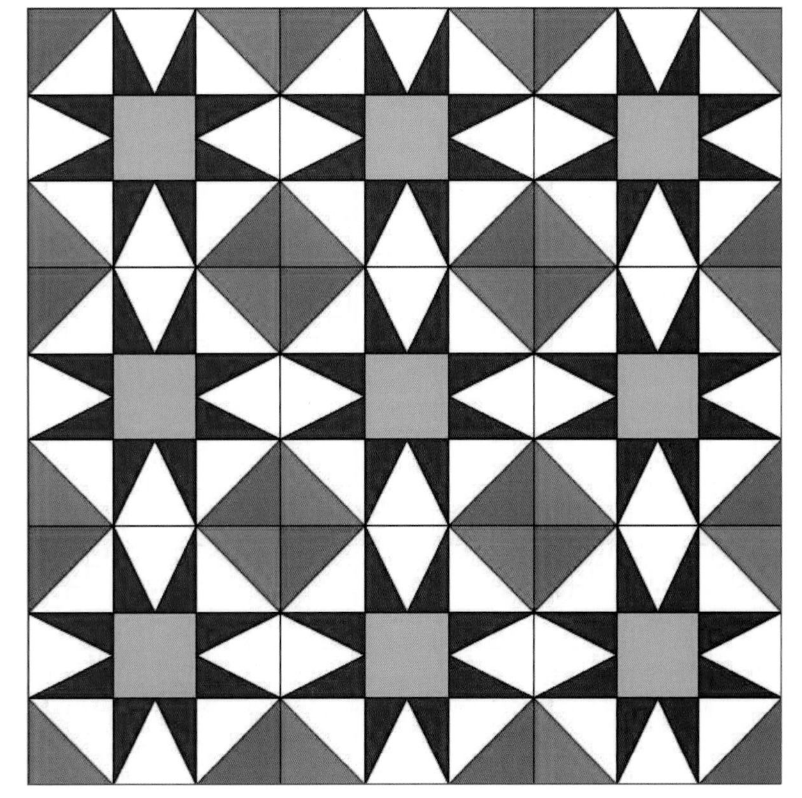

d. Star variation quilt

e. Irregular block

f. Quilt from irregular block

Machine piecing

Machine piecing, especially when combined with rotary cutting, enables you make multiple blocks very quickly. You are, however, confined to the house, or wherever your sewing machine is set up. Hand piecing is, of course, very portable and can be picked up and put down wherever and whenever you have time to do a couple of stitches.

The blocks we will use for our examples are familiar favourites - the stretched 9-patch, photo 1, and the Sawtooth Star, photo 2. These are simple, and related, blocks combining squares, rectangles and, in the case of the Sawtooth Star, half-square triangles.

1. Stretched 9-patch

2. Sawtooth Star

First prepare your fabric. It is up to you whether you pre-wash it or not. If you are making an heirloom quilt with deep colours that will be washed, then you may wish to pre-wash to prevent bleeding. Check whether the dye bleeds by wetting a piece of the fabric and ironing it on top of something white (an old tea towel for instance). If the colour transfers, then a pre-wash is probably a good idea. Whether you have washed it or not, your fabric will need to be pressed and, preferably, starched. The starch will help to keep its shape while you cut and stitch – especially important with triangles where you will be stitching along the bias.

Make sure your sewing machine is in good working order and that you have a new needle. If you've done more than 8 hours sewing with the current needle, it needs to be replaced. Wind a couple of bobbins with a suitable thread – neutral colour, and of the same weight/thickness as the top thread – as it can be infuriating to run out of bobbin thread half way down a long seam and have to stop long enough to wind a new bobbin.

Next check your rotary cutting equipment – is the cutter blade sharp, with no burrs? If not, then change it – blunt blades are not good news and can be hugely frustrating to work with.

You should be able to cut through two or three layers of fabric quickly and easily with no snags. If the new blade seems to be chewing the fabric, take it out and check it carefully – Chris's did this and she discovered she'd managed to buy and install two blades stuck together for the price of one. Once separated there were no further problems – and a free blade.

Check that your ¼" seam allowance really is ¼" as well. Do this by cutting 2, 1¼" strips and stitching them together with ¼" seam allowance. Make sure you are sitting at the machine so that you are looking directly along the seam line. Press carefully and measure the resulting paired strip. If it measures 2" your seam allowance is accurate; if not, measure the seam – if it is ¼" then check your pressing method - have you taken up some of the seam allowance in a tiny pleat? If your seam is not ¼", then you may need to adjust the needle position, your seating position (this explains why some days your seam allowance is spot on and other days it isn't), or your seam marker on the machine. Don't get yourself tied in knots over your seam allowance. If you can't get a ¼" then it just means that your piece will be slightly bigger, or slightly smaller, than the size given and you may have to adjust the measurements given for cutting borders or sashing, which is why it's usually best to leave cutting these to their exact size until you are ready to stitch them in place. Just try to keep a consistent seam allowance throughout a project.

The two blocks we'll be making should finish at 8". They are based on a 4-patch grid, so we will be working with 2" finished units. Before you start cutting out your fabric it makes sense to write a cutting plan – a note of what size and how many shapes to cut from each fabric – to put by your cutting mat. You can also write and stick a little 'Post-It™' note on each fabric. For added reassurance use a sticky note to mark the cutting line on your ruler for each strip or shape before you start to cut.

TIP

If you are going to a workshop it is always a good idea to take 2 or 3 pre-wound bobbins and to have a new machine needle and rotary cutter blade installed ready.

Stretched 9-Patch

For each Stretched 9-patch you will need to cut:
A centre square (fabric 1) – cut 1, 4½" square
Corner squares (either fabric 1 again or a different one, fabric 2) – cut 4, 2½" squares.
Rectangles (fabric 3) – cut 4, 2½" x 4½" rectangles (photo 3).
Notice we have added ½" to our basic 2" units to allow for a ¼" seam allowance all round. If you cut 4½" and 2½" strips from your fabrics first, photos 4 - 5, you can cut the pieces for several blocks at once. Look back at the

3. Cut pieces for Stretched 9-patch

4. Cut strips first

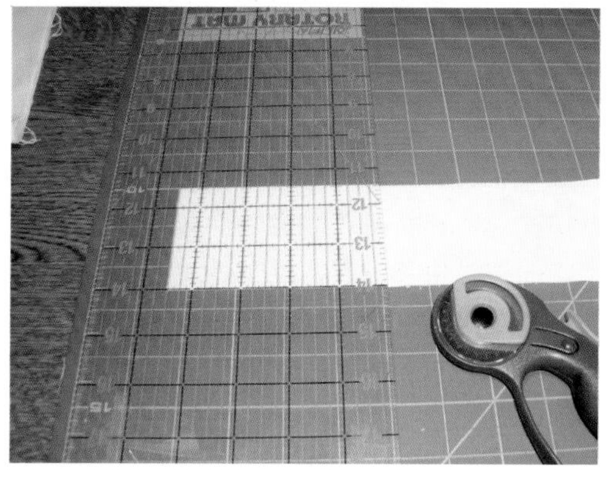

5. Subcut into rectangles

Equipment chapter where we discuss basic rotary cutting techniques. Remember, it is easier if you fold the fabric up because you have a shorter length to cut even though you have more thickness to cut through – if your blade is sharp, this shouldn't be a problem. Make sure the folds are lying flat on the board on the side nearest to you so that you cut through the folds first, not the raw edges.

6. Stretched 9-patch block layout

Lay your block(s) out so you can see how they go together, photo 6. If you are making more than one block lay them out one on top of another in a pile. If you are using different colour combinations then pile them up so the same colours are in each stack – it saves confusion.

7. Place first square on top of rectangle ...

Put your stack of blocks within easy reach of the sewing machine, sit yourself down, take a deep breath and pick up the first two pieces. We will start by stitching the small squares onto the ends of two of the rectangles. So pick up the top right hand square and place it right side down on the top rectangle, photo 7, matching the short raw edges, photo 8. Pick up the paired pieces by the raw edge you will be stitching (if you do this each time you lessen the risk of stitching along the wrong edge) and place it under the machine foot. Check the feed dogs are up, the stitch length is correct – we sometimes prefer to use a slightly longer stitch as it makes any unpicking easier – lower the presser foot and, checking that the raw edge is against your ¼" marker, photo 9, gently press on the foot pedal to start stitching. Don't hold the fabric firmly (or grip or tug it), just lightly rest a finger or two on it to guide it through the machine. In no time at all you will have reached the end of the seam (it is only 2½" after all). Stop stitching and without lifting the presser foot, pick up the next pair of square and rectangle to be stitched and feed them under the needle, photo 10. Start stitching again, just as before. And remember to keep breathing! Continue until you have finished stitching that seam on all your blocks. There is no need to start and finish your seams with knots or tiny stitches as you will fasten the seams when you stitch over them later. When you take the stitched pieces

8. ... and align raw edges

9. Place under machine foot

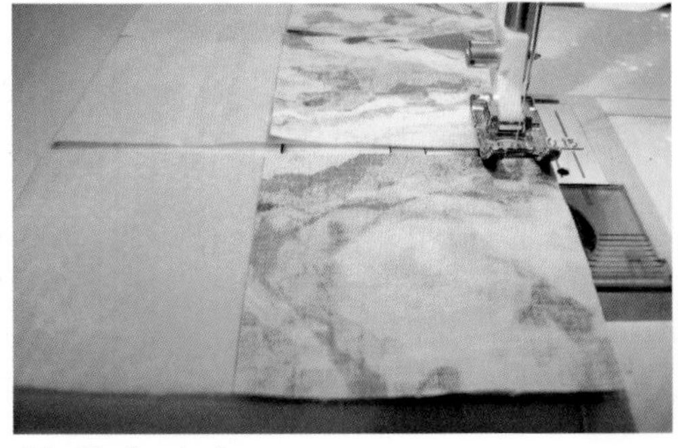

10. Chain piecing

out from the machine they will be joined together like a long streamer of little flags, photo 11. This method of machine piecing is known as 'chain piecing'. Just snip the threads between each piece, take them to the iron and press each seam to the side (to the darker fabric if possible), photos 12 - 15.

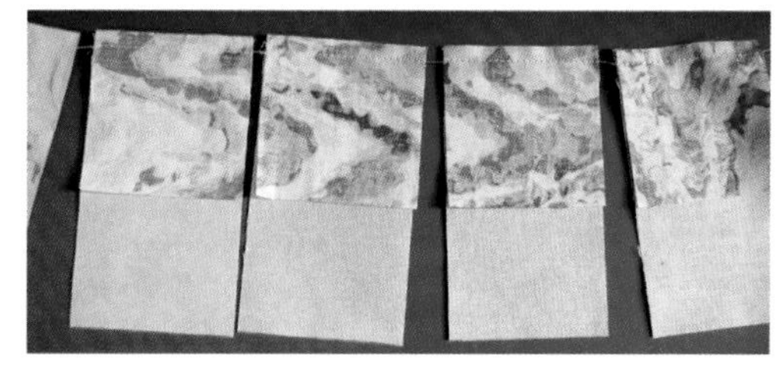

11. 'Flags'

12 -15 Press seams to one side

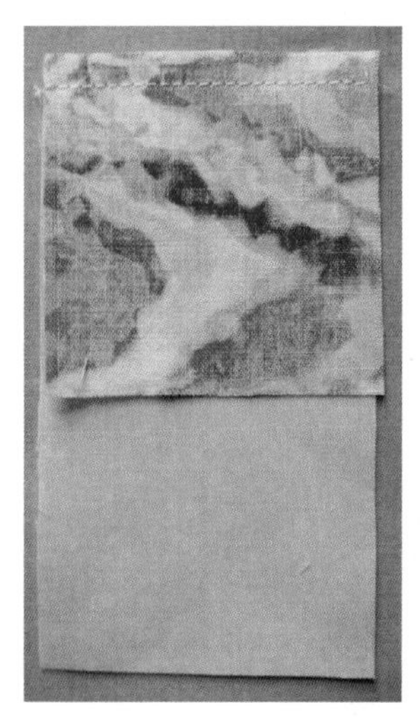

12. Ready to press

13. Press to darker fabric

14. Right side

14. Wrong side

Put the pressed pieces back in place in the block stack. Now stitch the bottom right hand squares to the bottom rectangles in the same way and place them back in the stack. Next stitch the small left-hand squares to the top and then to the bottom rectangles.

Now take the right-hand rectangle and place it right side down on the centre square, matching the raw edges as before, photo 16. Pick up the pair by this edge and stitch the seam as before, repeat with all the right hand rectangles; press the seams the other way to the small square seams, photos 17 - 20. In other words, if you pressed the seams towards the small squares and away from the rectangle, then press these seams towards the centre square and away from the rectangles again. This will make it much easier to join the rows together.

16. Align raw edges

17 – 20 Press to darker fabric

17. Ready to press

18. Press to darker fabric

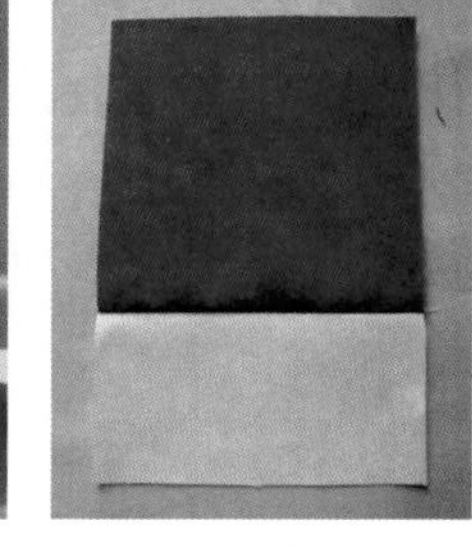

19. Right side

20. Wrong side

Finally stitch the left hand rectangles to the centre squares in the same way as before. When you place them back in the stack you should have three pieced rows ready to stitch, photo 21.

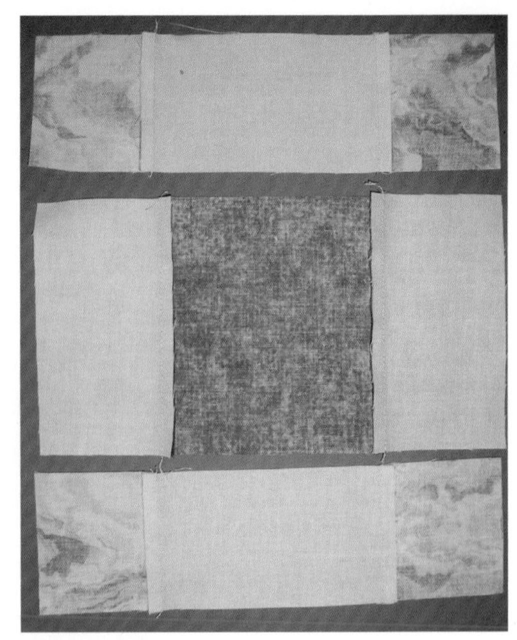

21. Wrong side of rows ready to stitch – note seams

Place the top row right side down on the middle row, photo 22, align the raw edges and check that the seams line up – if you have pressed the seams in the opposite direction they should butt up against each other, photo 23. If you wish you can put a pin at each seam intersection to hold them in place –pin at right-angles to the raw edge, photo 24. If you find that one piece is slightly longer than the other, place this piece at the bottom, against the feed dogs, to take advantage of the fact that they tend to gather the fabric slightly whereas the presser foot stretches slightly. Stitch all the blocks at this seam using the chain piecing method as before and press the seams – either to one side, or open, whichever way they wish to go. Place these almost finished blocks back in the stack, photo 25.

22. Align raw edges first two rows

23. Butted seams

24. Pin at seams

25. Two rows stitched

Finally flip the bottom row right side down on top of the middle row and stitch all these seams as before. Press carefully to complete each block, photo 1.

Reward yourself with a cuppa and a chocolate biscuit.

Sawtooth Star

The Sawtooth Star block, photo 2, is derived from the Stretched 9-patch – the side rectangles have been divided into three triangles. To make this block you can use the same fabrics as for the Stretched 9-patch or choose some different ones. You will want one for the centre square, one for the corner squares and the outer triangles (the 'background') and one for the smaller triangles – the 'star'.

For an 8" block you will need to cut:
1, 4½" square for the centre
4, 2½" 'background' squares for the corners
1, 5¼" 'background' square cut into four diagonally for the larger triangles, photo 26
4, 2⅞" squares, cut in two diagonally for the eight 'star' triangles, photos 27 - 28.

26. Quarter square triangles

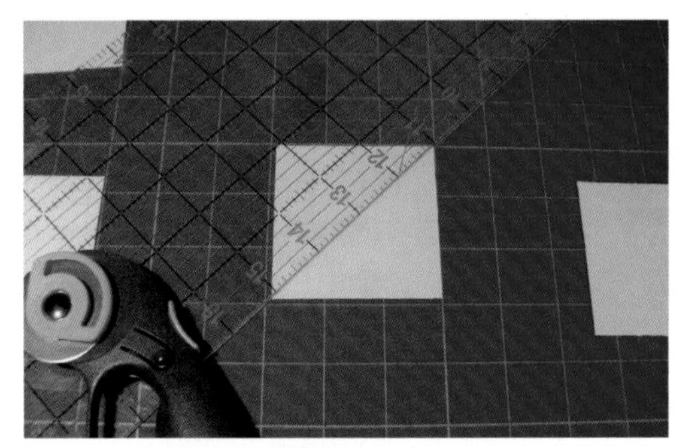

27. Cut squares in half …

28. … to make half-square triangles

As for the Stretched 9-patch, lay all the pieces for the block(s) out in the right order, photo 29. Start this time by stitching the triangles together to make the side rectangles.

Take the right hand top small triangle and place it right side down on the top background triangles, lining up the raw edges, photo 30. Pick it up, gently, by the side that you will be stitching and place it under the machine. Stitch the seam in exactly the same way as you stitched seams for the stretched 9-patch. You may find it helps, especially when stitching triangles, to have a piece of fabric as a 'leader' – one that you stitch along first before starting to stitch the triangles' seam, photo 31, - as this can prevent the point of the triangle from being chewed up in the throat-plate of the machine.

29. Sawtooth Star block layout

30. Align raw edges

31. Using a scrap 'leader'

> **TIP**
>
> *When you snip the threads at the end of each seam, don't trim them right back, leave a few twists as these will reduce the chances of the seam unravelling before you complete the quilt.*

Continue feeding the pieces through until you have stitched that seam on all the blocks you cut. Note that the sides you are stitching are on the bias. Handle them carefully, gently and as little as possible to avoid stretching them; starching the fabric well first should prevent a lot of this. Press the seam carefully to one side, making sure you are 'pressing' not 'ironing' so that you don't stretch the fabric, photo 32.

32. First triangle stitched

Now stitch the top left hand triangles to the top background triangles in the same way, photos 33 - 35.

33. Align raw edges

34. Second triangle stitched

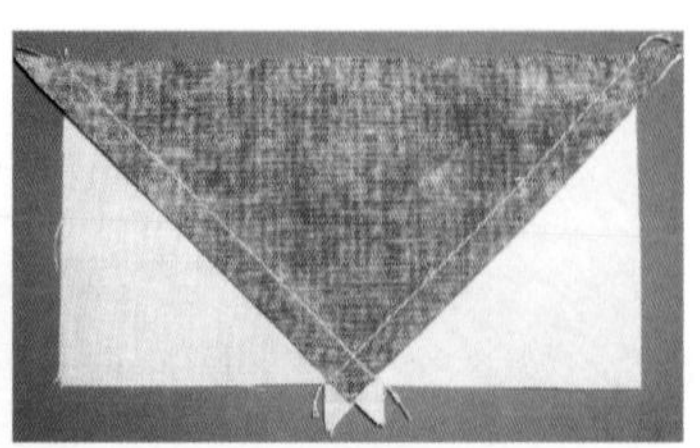

35. Wrong side of triangle piece

Stitch the triangles for the bottom and side rectangles as you did for the top rectangles. Press them carefully, trim off the 'ears', photo 36, and place them back in the stack, making sure you have the triangles facing the right way to make the star. It won't be a disaster if you sew them the wrong way round, you will have just sewn a different block.

36. Trim 'ears'

Now you have stitched the triangles into rectangles, the block you have laid out in front of you is the same as the Stretched 9-patch. Stitch it together following the instructions above for that block. When stitching the rectangles to the centre square, try to stitch the seam so it goes through the X formed by the triangles seams, photo 37, as this will ensure you get a nice sharp point, photo 38. Press seams carefully towards the unpieced squares, wherever possible, until the block is complete, photo 2. Reward yourself with another cuppa and a chocolate biscuit while admiring your handiwork.

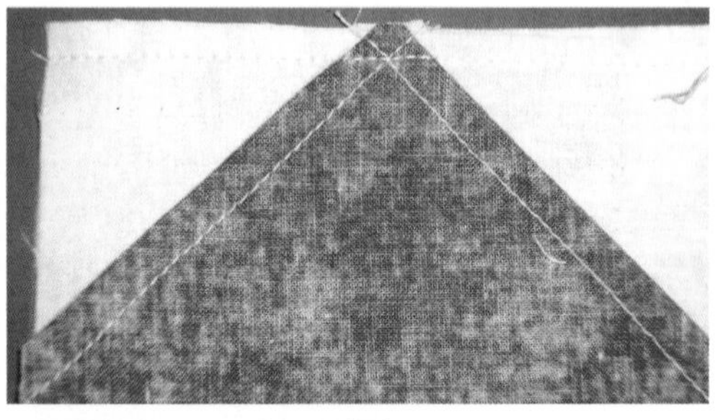

37. Stitch seam through X ...

38. ...to ensure sharp points

39. Sawtooth Star rows, ready to complete

Hand piecing

Sometimes we think that hand piecing, like hand appliqué, suffers from being regarded as one of those 'love it or hate it' techniques but over the past year or so it seems that interest in hand piecing has increased very significantly. Of course, it has the advantage of being ultra portable and it really is amazing how much you can accomplish by stitching in 'lost' time, waiting for planes, trains, buses, doctors and other appointments. Barbara finds it difficult to leave home even to go shopping without taking a small bag containing a minimum of two projects with her! You don't have to take it to that extreme but if you make sure that you (almost) always have a bag of basics with you we think you'll be surprised at how productive you can be for very little effort.

Barbara's tips for productive stitching at home or away

- My travelling bag usually contains two blocks' worth of cut and marked pieces, two needles, four pins, reel of thread, small scissors, thimble and a small chunk of beeswax, photo 1.

- Keep it simple and choose a block you like and fabrics you like. Banish all thoughts of time and a finished project of whatever size. This is about the process of stitching more than the product.

- Make the necessary templates and keep them together clearly marked.

1. Contents of Barbara's sewing bag

- I also keep my starting fabrics all together and make suitable additions as I use up the first choices.

- I like to mark up and cut enough pieces for several blocks at once and just savour the delights of stitching in gaps during the day. You can decide much further down the road what you could make with the growing collection of blocks.

- It takes surprisingly little time to hand piece a block – once you are familiar with your chosen process and have your bag of stitching always within reach it's possible to complete a block a day, and certainly in a week........and there are 52 weeks in a year which might be enough for a whole quilt!, photo 2.

2. Enough blocks for a quilt

Requirements for hand piecing

Here's our list of what we think you need for successful hand piecing.

- pins – we like the fine flower head pins
- small scissors
- fabric scissors
- cotton sewing thread – a neutral colour will work for most situations e.g. dove grey, dark cream
- needles, use either sharps or maybe even betweens
- a pincushion is useful
- templates – plastic or card are usual choices
- fabric marker – light colour and regular pencil
- fabric of course!
- fine grade sandpaper – we glued a sheet of this onto an acrylic kitchen chopping board which works very well – this is to help keep templates and fabric from slipping as you are marking out and also serves as a small work board.

Fabric preparation

Pre-wash fabric, if you wish, and press well. If you have plenty of time you might also consider spray starching the fabric to help keep it stable whilst you are marking and cutting.

Making and using templates

Template materials

Trace any templates provided and glue the tracing to thin card – old cereal boxes are fine.

If you want to a more durable template, or to position a motif (so you need a transparent template) use template plastic and trace directly onto it.

Label each template, stating the name of the block, the size, and whether the template includes a seam allowance or not.

Templates for each block can be kept together in an envelope.

Seam lines

The templates provided may not have the seam lines marked.

For machine piecing you may need to add the seam allowance to each template; the lines you draw on the fabric around these templates are then cutting lines.

For hand piecing, cut the templates without a seam allowance – the lines you draw on the fabric will be the sewing lines.

Make sure you state on the template whether or not you have added a seam allowance.

Cutting out

Make and cut out your templates carefully as any inaccuracy here will multiply several fold as you make the quilt.

Take care with templates that are not symmetrical – mark them so that you know which side to place down on the fabric.

Hand piecing over papers

This is where many of us began (or continued), often with the much maligned hexagons. We can both remember when this was regarded as the only 'proper' way to do patchwork – thankfully the quilt police now have a much wider field of interest and have accepted machine work! Piecing over papers, done with care, has a high accuracy rating and is what is says – fabric is tacked/basted over paper shapes and stitched together with neat whipstitch. This method is great for working in batches when time permits. For instance you could use a short time slot of 5 - 30 minutes to mark and cut a batch of papers. These would then be ready to use for marking and cutting out fabric shapes and stacking them ready for tacking which might fill up another 5 - 30 minute slot. Tacked shapes can be strung together on a knotted length of thread to keep them tidy and accounted for until you are ready to start stitching shapes together.

Piecing over papers is most often associated with single shapes e.g. hexagons, diamonds and the worked example we show here is the familiar hexagon rosette, photos 3 and 4.
Make accurate template(s) for the required shape(s) from a firm material such as plastic or lightweight card.

3. Antique hexagon quilt

4. Same quilt, showing papers

Use the template and a fine permanent marker/pencil to trace the shape(s) onto paper – this can be regular A4 copier paper or if you want to follow in the tradition, use whatever is to hand – bills, school exercise books, letters, glossy magazines. Alternatively you can cut to the chase and purchase ready cut papers – check your local quilt shop and the small ads in quilting magazines. You might like to try marking your chosen shapes onto freezer paper – cut out the shapes and dry iron them onto the WS of the fabric before basting the fabric into place. If you are careful and baste through the fabric only, not the paper, these paper shapes would be re-usable two or three times more …

Mark and cut out the required number of paper shapes, photo 5.

Place or pin the papers onto WS of your chosen fabric and carefully cut around the papers leaving a generous ¼" seam allowance on all sides, photo 6.

5. Ready to start

6. Pieces cut

Begin with a knot and finish with a couple of small backstitches. Use a neutral thread to tack the fabric into position over the paper shape with short straight stitches. It is advisable to have stitch securing each major fold of the fabric, photos 7, 8 and 9.

7. Tack folds

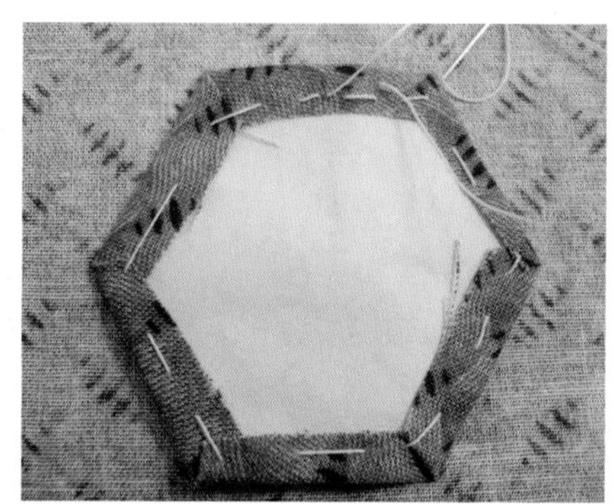

8. Tacking complete

9. Rosette tacked

TIP

You can have a lot of fun making new effects by "fussycutting" fabrics for paper piecing, particularly the standard classic shapes e.g. hexagons and diamonds, photo A, – position each of the papers over the same portion of the fabric pattern and admire the stitched result!

A. Fussy cut diamonds

10 a – d . Overcast stitch

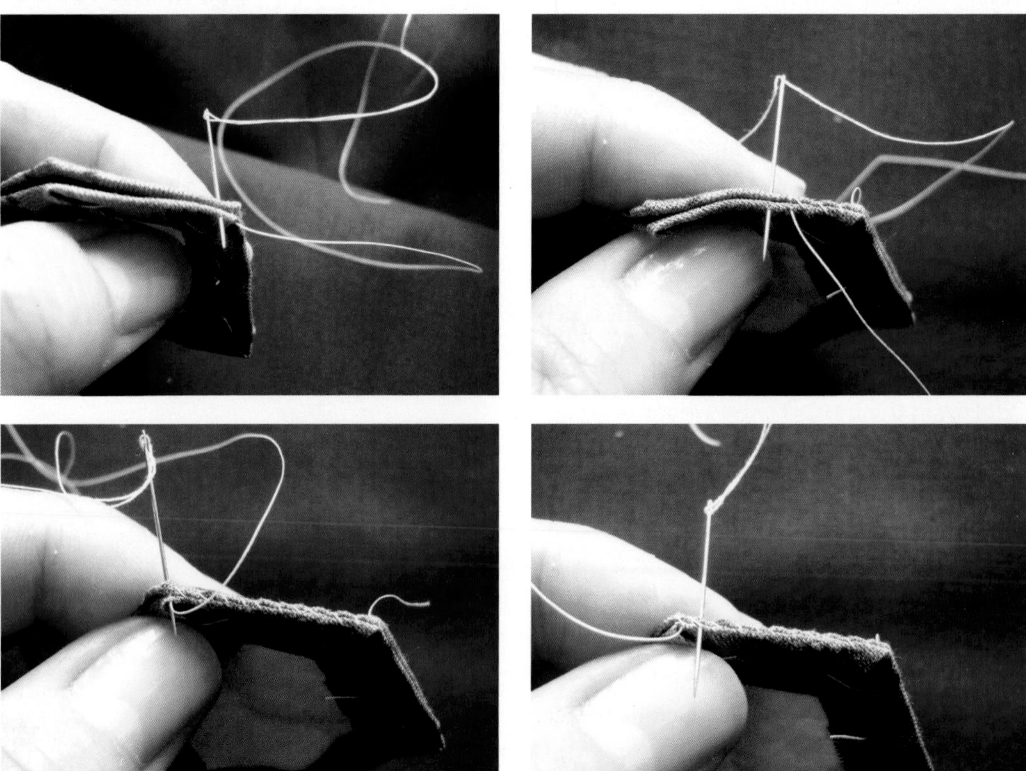

To join patches together use a matching or neutral thread according to your preference. Knot the end of your thread and begin in the seam allowance of the shape facing you – you will have the two shapes RS together and then continue with a neat whip or overcasting stitch, photo 10a – d. You will be stitching through the fold of fabric at the paper's edge rather than through the paper. Finish the seam by working three or four stitches in reverse direction along the seam just sewn, photo 11.

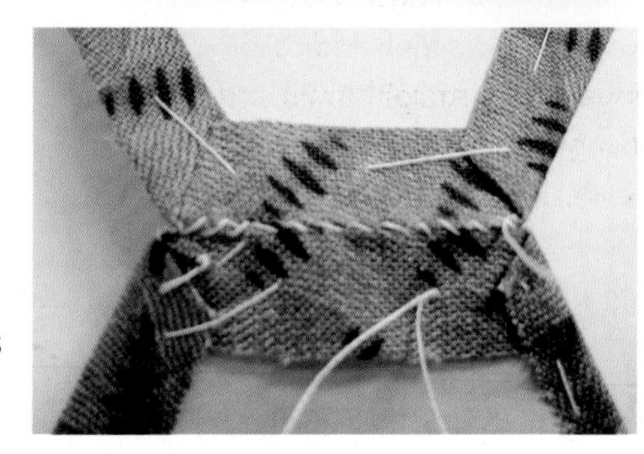

11. Completed seam

As for all piecing you can often make things manageable by working in small units and systematically building up to something larger, photos 12a – c.

Piecing over papers does not necessarily have to be restricted to mosaic or one shape work. You can use this method for most blocks with straight seams – some of us have distant memories of making our first Mariner's Compass block 'over papers' and it always used to be considered the most accurate piecing technique for complex work.

12a - c. Stitch rosette in rows

Piecing without papers

For this traditional handpiecing method you will need to make templates from a suitable material for each of the shapes you require. We think it's a good idea to identify the templates by labelling with a permanent marker and, if there's room, noting how many of each shape you need to cut, photo 13. Before computer quilt programs we used to make a sketch of the block to identify the templates, now we just print out a reference block from our favourite program (EQ since you ask) and keep that in the project bag.

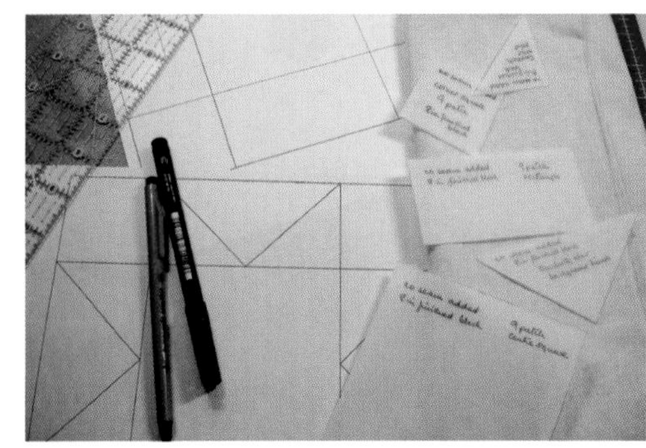

13. Marked templates

Carefully mark around the template on WS of fabric – this will be the stitching line.
A quick word about grainline here – it is worth taking a little extra time to position the templates so that the grainline of the fabric helps to keep the finished work as stable as possible and minimise distortion. Notice where the arrows are in dia. 1, of the Sawtooth Star – all the outside edges are on the straight grain, so the large triangle is drawn with the long edge on the straight grain and the smaller triangles are drawn with the short edges on the straight grain, photo 14.

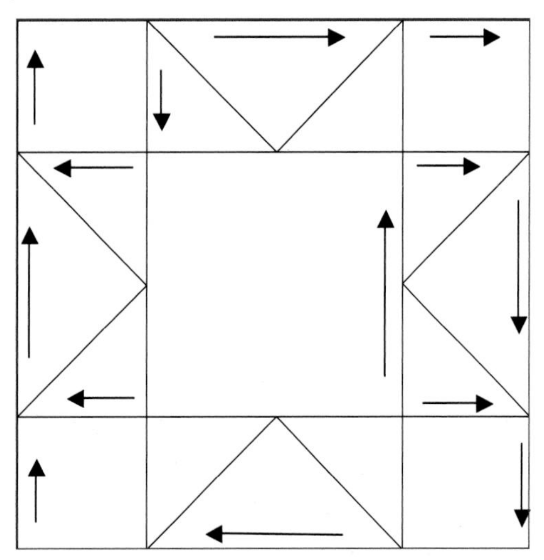

dia. 1. Block layout, showing grain lines

Cut out the shapes leaving a generous ¼" seam allowance on all sides, photo 15.

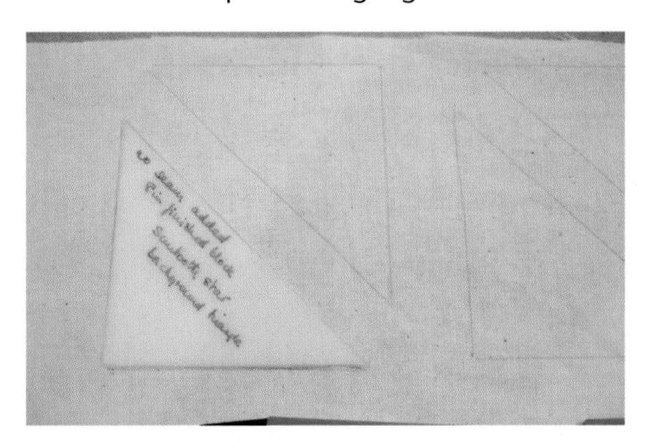

14. Draw round templates

15. Cut out

Keep track of the cut pieces – we like to mark out several blocks worth of shapes onto fabric and then cut the pieces for one block only and stitch this block before cutting any further pieces. Alternatively you can string patches together in groups, or keep them in separate small bags.

The example here is one of our favourite blocks – Sawtooth Star – which you may remember from the machine piecing chapter and we'll be following the same well-established principle of building up from small units.

With RS together line up the marked seam allowances on the small and larger triangles. Use pins to check your accuracy and also to secure the pieces in their correct alignment.
Begin with a knot in the seam allowance and make your first stitch around the securing pin.

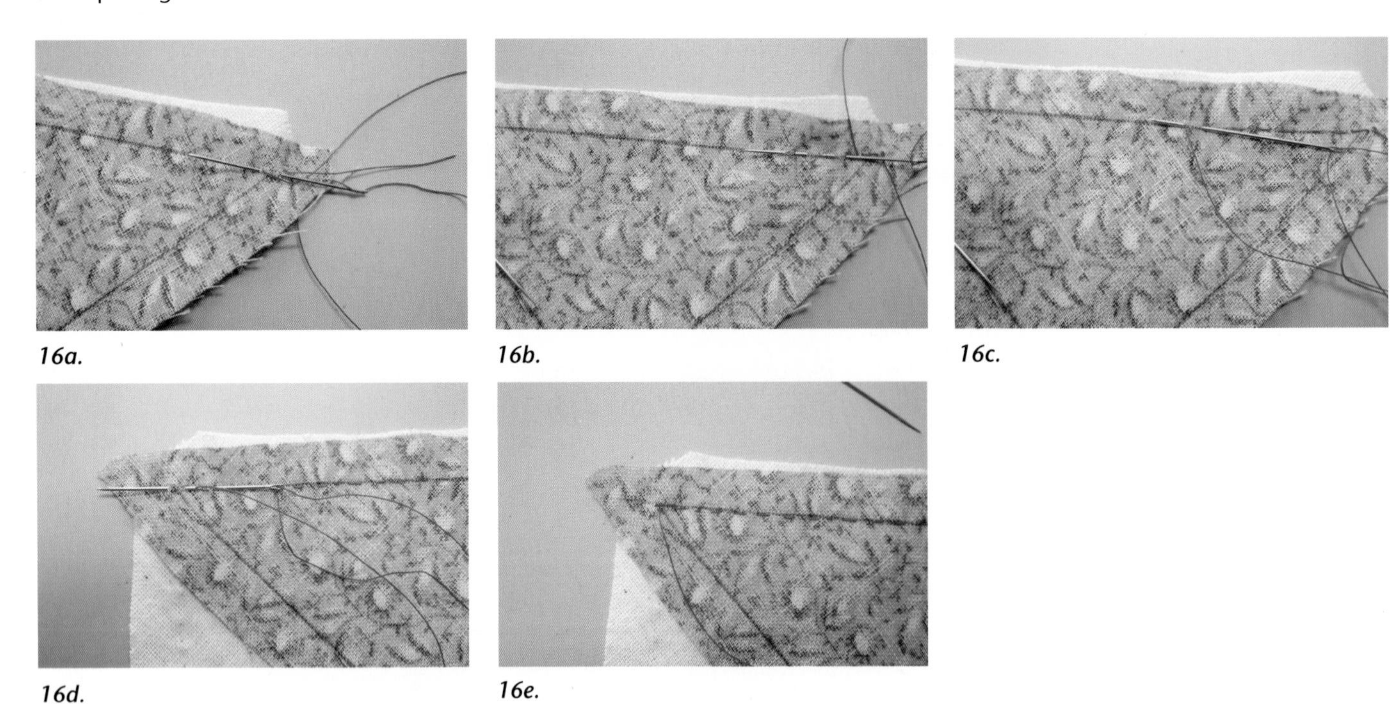

16a. *16b.* *16c.* *16d.* *16e.*

Make small running stitches through the two layers and check from time to time that you are still 'on line'. Add in a few backstitches at regular intervals, say every three or four stitches – this is not strictly necessary but it makes us all feel so much better! Finish with a couple of backstitches and then an extra couple of backstitches into the seam allowance for good measure before cutting the thread, photos 16a – e.

Finger press the small triangle into position and proceed to position and pin the second triangle ready for stitching.

With hand piecing it is customary ***NOT*** to stitch across and over seam allowances unlike machine piecing. Instead the convention is to stitch ***through*** seams. Begin with the knot in the seam allowance of the small triangle facing you. Take the needle through to the back holding the seam allowance to one side, push it through the seam allowance and then through to the front of the work again before beginning to stitch along the marked line, photos 17a – d.

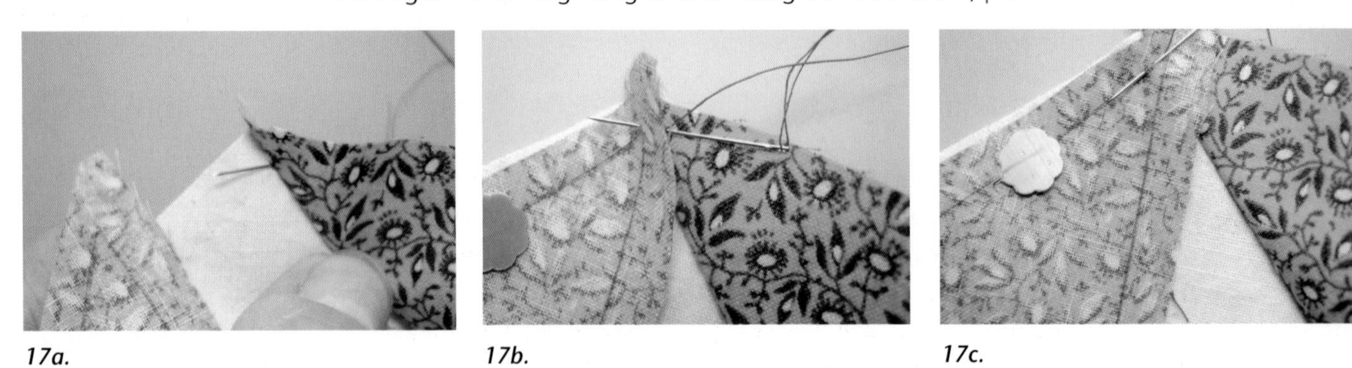

17a. *17b.* *17c.*

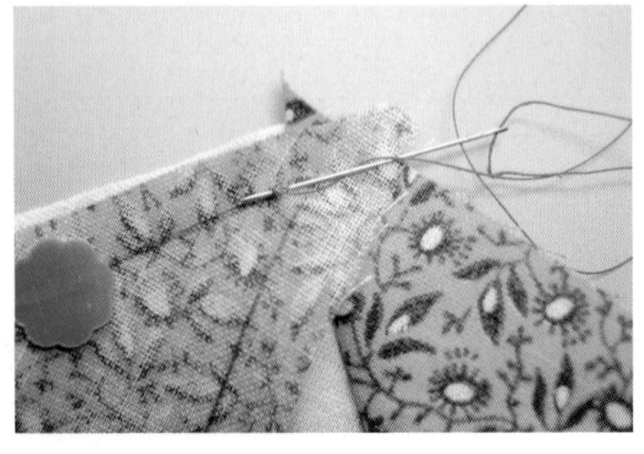

17d.

Working through the seams in this way means that you have secured the seams sufficiently and the seam allowances are still free to be pressed in any direction. Stitching across seam allowances as if you were doing machine piecing is awkward to do and lumpy in finish.

Make up a total of four Flying Geese units, photo 18, in the same way.

18.

Position, pin and stitch a square onto each end of two of the Flying Geese units – remember to stitch through the seam allowance rather than across it.

Position, pin and stitch the two remaining Flying Geese units to opposite sides of the large square – here you will negotiate the centre seams where the three triangles meet, photos 19a – c.

19a.

19b.

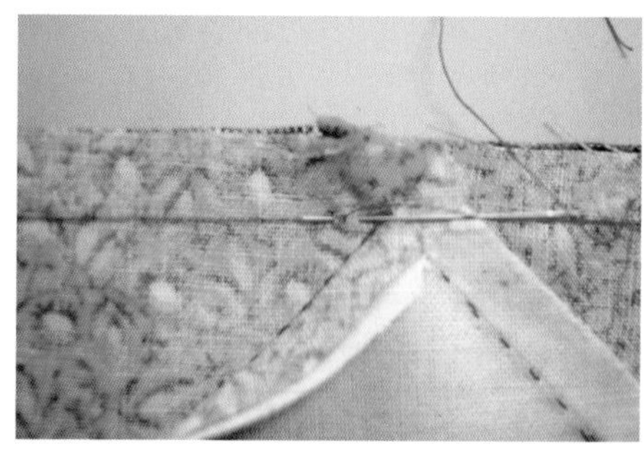

19c.

Take your time to work your way through and around this point – it isn't difficult at all, it just needs some attention in following a sequence.

Position and pin the stitched units as shown in dia. 2, and sew the two long seams required to complete the block.

dia. 2. Block layout, piecing sequence

Piecing without papers II

The third hand piecing technique we want to include is largely the same as the American piecing just described but with some important differences.

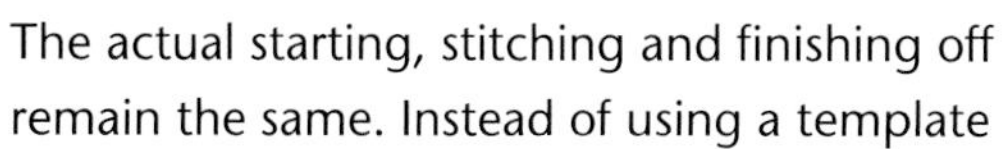

The actual starting, stitching and finishing off remain the same. Instead of using a template which is the actual finished size of the shape you will be using a template or measurements which, as for machine piecing, is the actual size plus ¼" seam allowance on all sides – for a 3" finished square you would cut a 3½" square. So with this method you will be cutting first and marking the seam later rather than the traditional way of marking the seam first and cutting second. The benefit of working this way is that you can use your rotary cutting skills to quickly and accurately cut lots of shapes from starched and stacked fabric. To prepare the shapes for stitching you can use one of those hugely useful ¼" quilter's rulers and mark the start and finish of the seam with a dot on the WS of the palest fabric. One handy tip Barbara picked up from well-known US teacher Billie Lauder is to use an ultra-fine point Pigma pen as a marker for this no-template method. The ink is permanent and should not bleed and the pen is fine enough to make clearly visible dots and lines. Join up the dots with a ruled line and you're ready to stitch. The stitching is the same simple short running stitch described above so it's really easy and your project is still totally portable.

TIP

Warning *– check your marker on a piece of scrap before using. Use either a pencil, or a marker that does not bleed to mark your dots and join them. Photo 20 shows the use of a pencil at the top of the square and an ordinary marking pen – which has bled – at the bottom.*

20.

Quick piecing

Stitch before you cut!

Quick piecing is the name given to the technique of stitching fabric before you cut it. It saves time, fabric and frayed temper – particularly for pieces on the bias. This is particularly true for half-square and quarter-square triangles which can be stitched along the bias before being cut. In this chapter we'll look at quick-piecing several essential patchwork units before considering how cutting and stitching strips together can speed up your piecing. Quick piecing and strip piecing techniques should also give you some new ideas for using that jelly roll sitting on the shelf!

Half square triangles

Single units

Determine the size of the finished square unit ie two triangles stitched together – let's say you want a 3" finished square.
Add ⅞" to this measurement - this will be 3⅞".
Cut squares to this measurement, mark one diagonal on WS of each lighter square.
Put 2 squares RS together.
Stitch ¼" on either side of the marked diagonal line, dia. 1a.
Cut on the marked line, press as stitched, then press to RS with seam allowance in appropriate direction (usually towards darker fabric to avoid any show-through).
Trim "ears" off units.

dia. 1 Half-square triangles

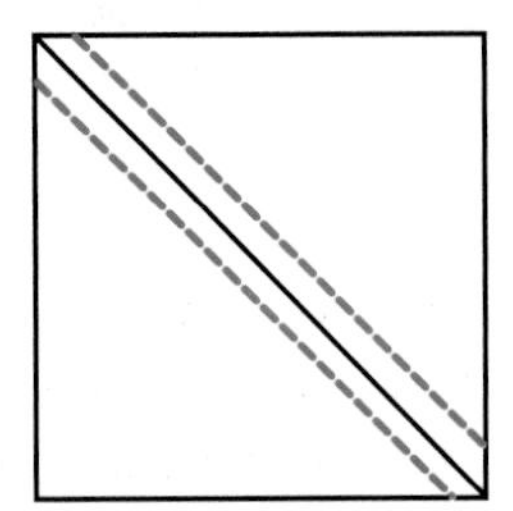

a. Mark and stitch ¼" either side of diagonal

Multiple units

Determine the number of units you require and the size of the finished square – add ⅞" to this finished size.
On the WS of one fabric draw a grid of squares of this measurement making sure that the total number of squares in the grid is the number you require.
Carefully mark in diagonals in one direction only in all squares of the grid. This will be your cutting line.
For best accuracy also mark lines ¼" either side of the diagonals. These will be your stitching lines, dia. 1b.
To avoid any possible confusion when stitching you may find it helpful to make some sort of identifying mark, such as arrowheads, on these lines.
Layer and pin both fabrics RS together.
Stitch along marked stitching lines.
Cut apart on all remaining lines to yield requisite number of squares.
Press and trim as described above.

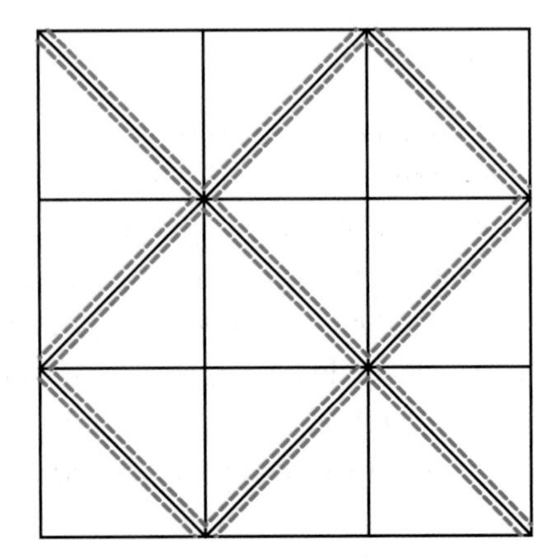

b. Mark and stitch multiple diagonals

Quarter square triangles

Single units

Determine the finished size of the quarter square triangle unit required and add 1¼" to this measurement.
Cut 2 squares of the size required.
On WS of lightest fabric mark both diagonals On one diagonal only mark ¼" line on both sides of the line, dia. 2a.
Put squares RS together.
Using a short/medium stitch length, stitch on the ¼" lines. Press flat. Cut apart on remaining marked lines to give 4 triangle units.
Press carefully, distortion is easy.
Arrange units into squares and join together, dia. 2b.

dia. 2 Quarter-square triangles

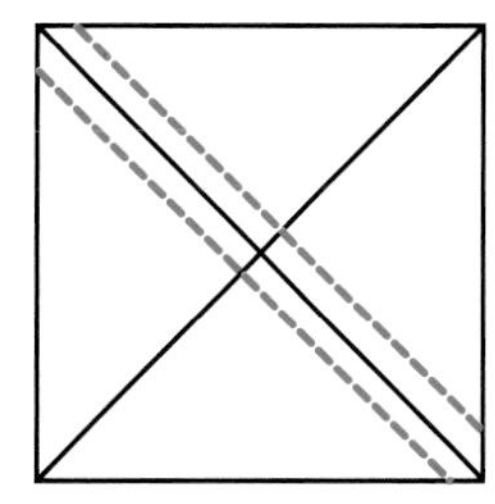

a. Mark both diagonals and stitch ¼" away from one

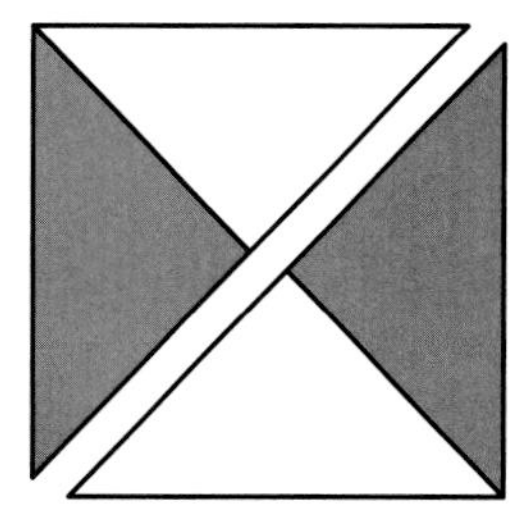

b. Stitch pairs of units to complete square.

Two units

Make 2 half-square triangle units.
Place them right sides together, reversing the colours.
Mark the opposite diagonal to the stitching on the top square, dia. 2c.
Stitch ¼" either side of this marked line, dia. 2d.
Cut apart.

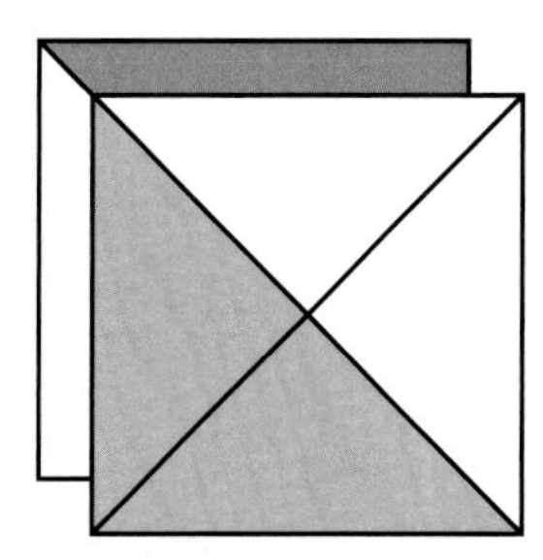

c. Mark diagonal, place squares WS together

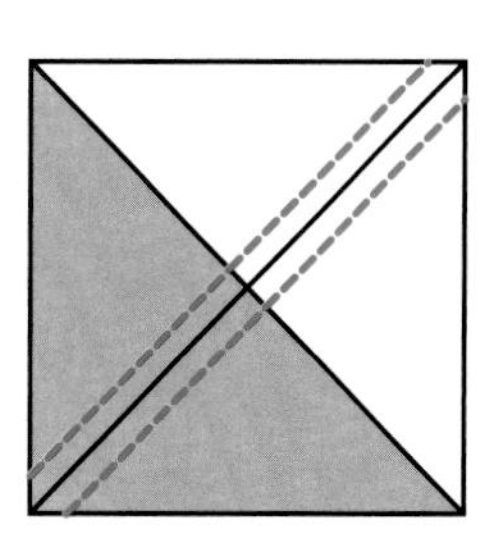

d. Stitch ¼" either side of marked diagonal

Multiple units

Layer 2 chosen fabrics RS together.
Mark a grid of squares on WS of palest fabric.
Determine the size of the squares by adding 1¼" to the size of finished units required.
Mark ¼" lines on both sides of one set of diagonals.
Using a short/medium stitch length, stitch all marked ¼" lines, dia. 2e.
Press flat.
Cut apart on remaining marked lines.
Press units carefully.
Arrange into squares and join together.
Press again.

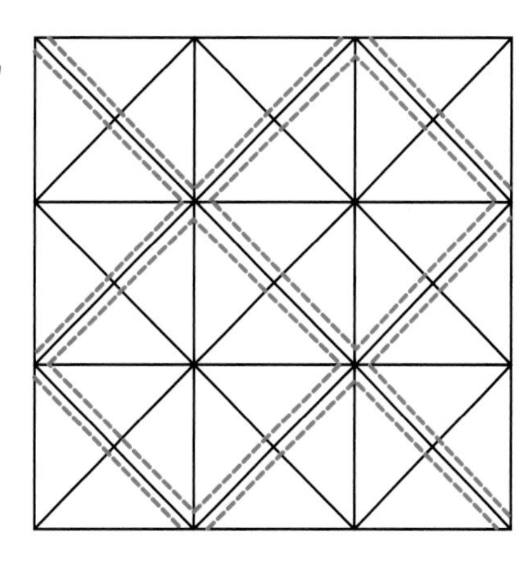

e. Mark and stitch multiple diagonals

Half-square/quarter-square triangle

These are made in a similar way to the double quarter-square triangles units.
Make a half-square triangle unit.
Pair with a plain square with the diagonal marked on the wrong side – ensure this marked line is in the opposite direction to the stitching on the triangle square, dia. 3a.
Stitch ¼" either side of the marked line, dia. 3b.
Cut apart, dia. 3c.

dia. 3 Half-square/quarter-square triangle

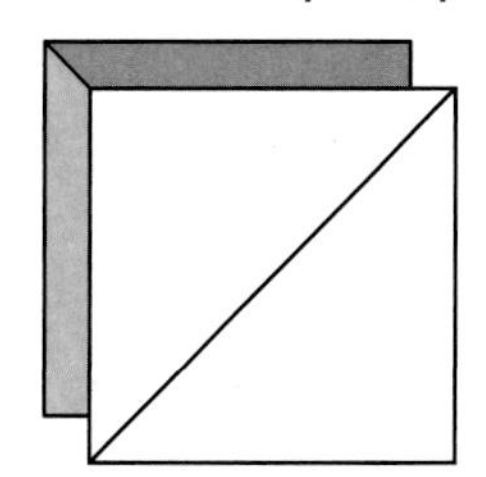

a. Place triangle square WS together with marked plain square

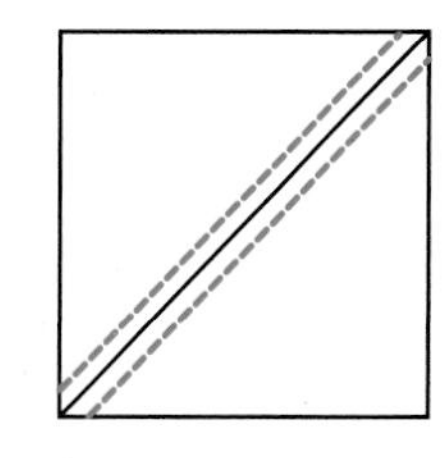

b. Stitch ¼" either side marked line

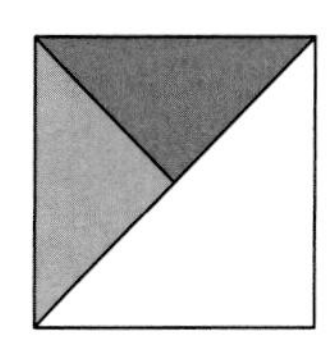

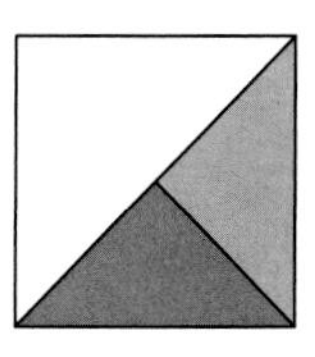

c. Cut apart

dia. 4 Square in a Square

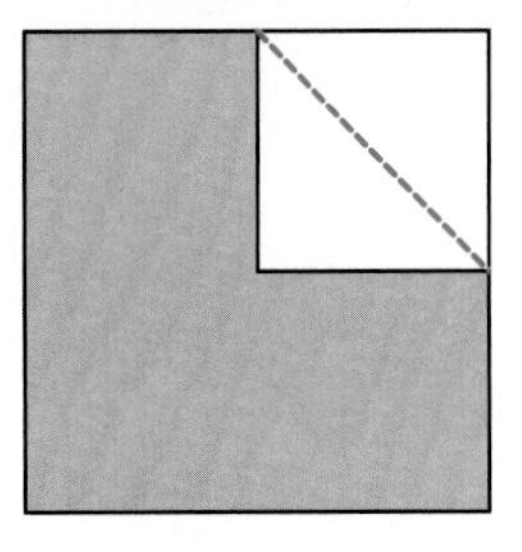

a. Place first small square in corner, stitch on the diagonal

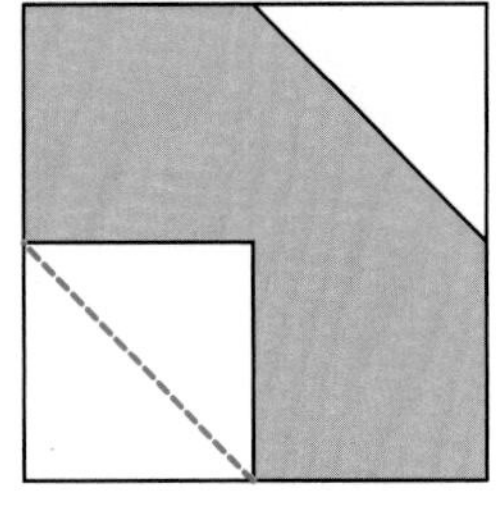

b. Flip triangle back. Repeat with other corners

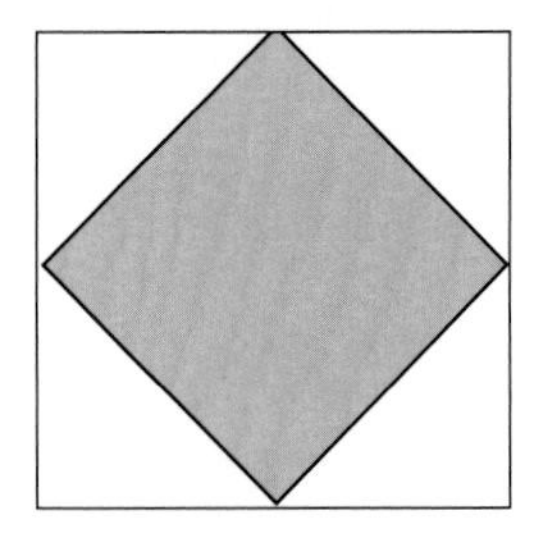

c. Complete unit

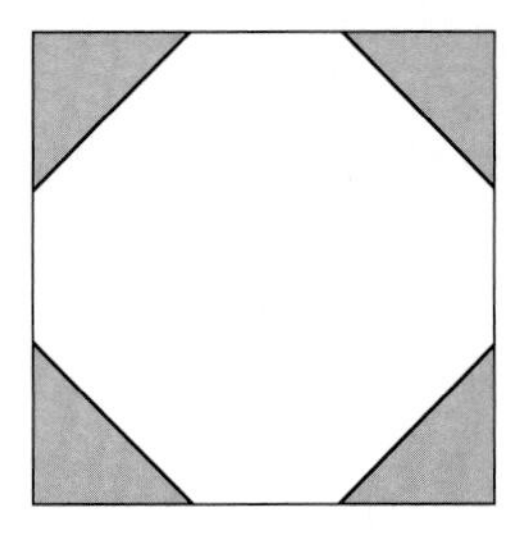

d. Snowball unit

Square in a Square

For the centre (on point) square, cut a square the finished size of the unit plus ½".

For the corner triangles cut 4 squares the finished size of the triangle plus ⅞". Mark the diagonal on the wrong side of each square either with a pencil or by lightly pressing a crease.

Place the first triangle square on the large square in one corner, matching raw edges – ensure marked line runs across the corner of the large square.

Stitch along marked line, dia. 4a.

Flip the triangle back to cover the corner. You may trim the excess fabric from the corner at this point if you wish.

Repeat with remaining 3 corners, dia. 4b, to complete the unit, dia. 4c.

This method may also be used to make a Snowball unit, dia. 4d.

dia. 5 Flying Geese

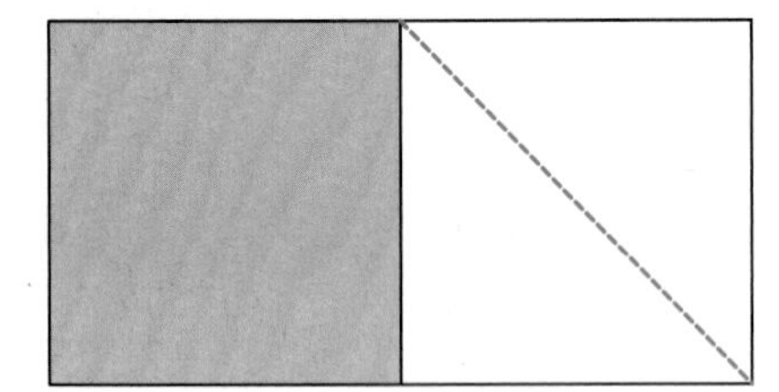

a. Place first square and stitch on the diagonal

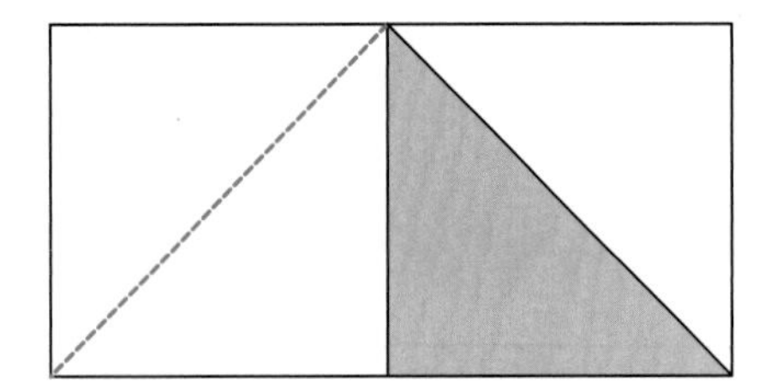

b. Flip and repeat with other square.

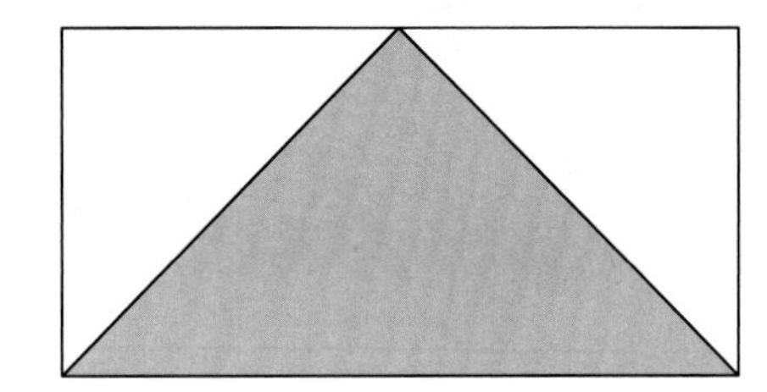

c. Complete unit.

Flying Geese

Single units

The stitch and flip method for Square in a Square can be used for Flying Geese units too.

For the centre (large) triangle (the goose) cut a rectangle ½" bigger than finished size of the Flying Geese unit.

For the background triangles cut squares ⅞" larger than finished short side of the unit.

Mark diagonals, place on one corner of rectangle aligned with 3 edges of rectangle.

Stitch across diagonal line, dia. 5a. Flip. Trim excess fabric away leaving ¼" seam allowance.

Repeat with other corner, dia. 5b.

Trim excess fabric if desired and press, dia. 5c.

Multiple units (4 geese at once)

For 4 Flying Geese units you will need:

1 square of goose fabric cut 1¼" larger than finished length of Flying Geese units.

4 squares of background fabric cut ⅞" inch larger than short sides of units.

Align 2 background squares (orange) at opposite corners of goose square (black), photo 1, and clip corners, photo 2.

Mark diagonal across both background squares, photo 3.

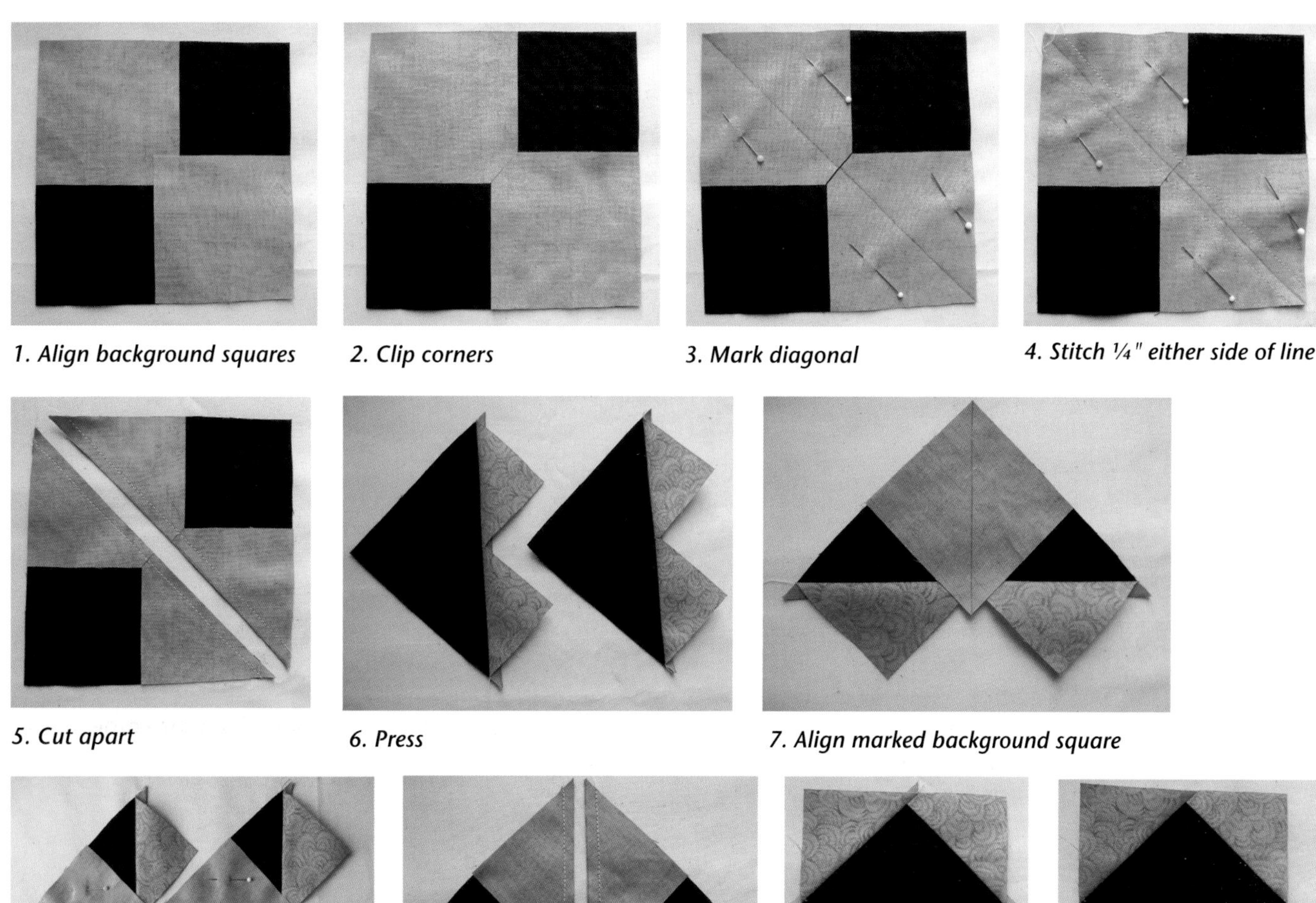

1. Align background squares *2. Clip corners* *3. Mark diagonal* *4. Stitch ¼" either side of line*

5. Cut apart *6. Press* *7. Align marked background square*

8. Stitch ¼" either side of line *9. Cut apart* *10. Press* *11. Trim 'ears'*

Stitch ¼" from both sides of marked line, photo 4.
Press flat then cut on diagonal line between the two lines of stitching, photo 5.
Carefully press small triangles away from the goose square, photo 6.
Align a third background square with the remaining "empty" corner of each goose square, photo 7. Mark the diagonal and stitch ¼" from both sides of this marked line, photo 8.
Press flat before cutting apart on the marked diagonal line, photo 9. Press completed unit, photo 10. Repeat this step for the remaining unit and trim 'ears', photo 11.

Strip piecing

Squares and rectangles

Strip piecing is a quick piecing technique - strips are stitched together before being cut apart into various shapes – squares, rectangles, triangles and diamonds. This is a quick, easy and accurate way to make a variety of patchwork designs and it's a technique we really enjoy. It eliminates the need to make templates and mark round the shapes on each piece of fabric, and it can look dramatic and complex – lots of result for relatively little effort! But there is just one note of caution before you get going with your own speed piecing project - take care not to get too carried away by the speed of the whole thing and neglect the need to pay attention to keeping a consistent seam allowance throughout the project.

Of course, cutting strips is so much quicker and more accurate with the rotary cutter, and it's a great way to gain confidence and experience using this important tool.

We would recommend that you starch your fabric before cutting as this helps to keep its shape and prevent fraying.

Many of these simple blocks and units make good alternate blocks – somewhere for the eye to rest in a more complicated design.
Let's look first at what you can do with just two strips. Choose two fabrics which contrast – a light and dark, say – and that you don't mind sacrificing for these experiments.

dia. 6. Windmill

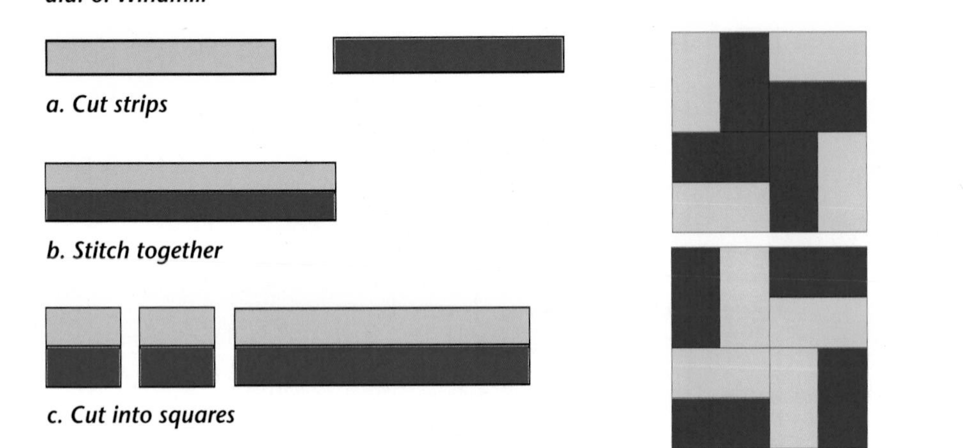

a. Cut strips

b. Stitch together

c. Cut into squares

d. Join squares

e. 4 blocks put together

Just two strips
Windmill
Cut 1, 2½" strip of each colour, dia. 6a. Join the two strips together using a ¼" seam and press the seam towards the darker colour, dia. 6b. Slice this new strip into 4½" segments, dia. 6c. Join these square segments to make a new block, Windmill, dia. 6d. Four of these blocks put together are shown in dia. 6e. Your sliced segments need to be 4½" along all four sides to fit together accurately. If your cutting and measuring were accurate, you may need to check that your seam allowance is exactly ¼" and adjust it accordingly if not. You can adjust your seam allowance by moving the position of your needle or adjusting the guide line on the right hand edge, or even by something as simple as adjusting your position in front of the machine so that your eyeline is directly along the raw edge you are stitching.

> **TIP**
>
> *Making a simple block like this can be a good test of your accuracy in cutting and measuring.*

Four Patch
Cut 1, 2½" strip of each colour, dia. 7a. Join the two strips together using a ¼" seam and press the seam towards the darker colour, dia. 7b. Slice this new strip into 2½" segments, dia. 7c. Stitch these segments together in pairs to make four-patch units, dia. 7d, with a finished size of 4". Match the seams for greater accuracy – one should be pressed one way and one the other, dia. 7e.

dia. 7 4-patch

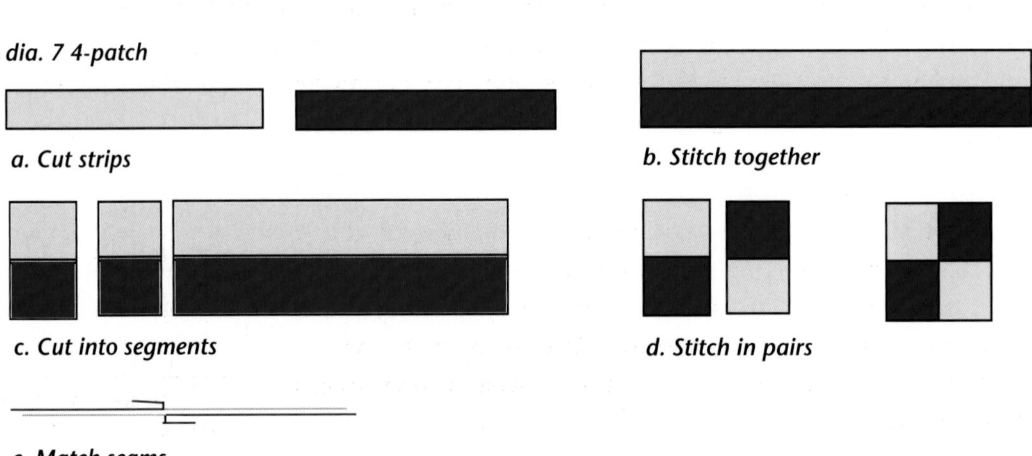

a. Cut strips

b. Stitch together

c. Cut into segments

d. Stitch in pairs

e. Match seams

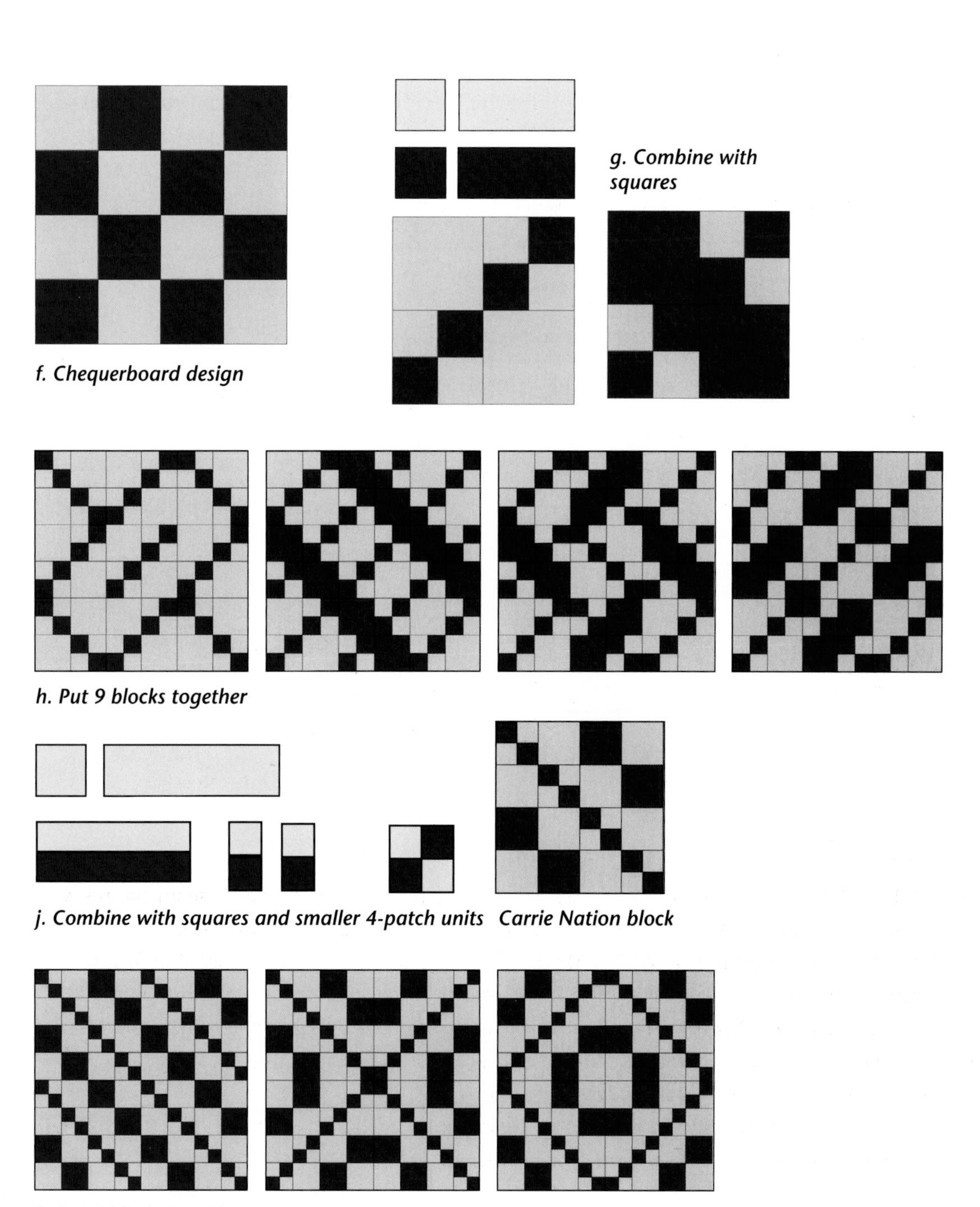

f. *Chequerboard design*

g. Combine with squares

h. Put 9 blocks together

j. Combine with squares and smaller 4-patch units

Carrie Nation block

k. Put 4 blocks together

Several of these units joined together will make a chequerboard design, dia. 7f. Or you can combine them with squares cut from a 4½" strip to make this block, dia. 7g. Putting several of these blocks together, especially using the two different colourings or rotating blocks, can make quite pleasing designs, dia. 7h. Or you can combine 4-patch units with squares cut from a 2½" wide strip and smaller 4-patch units cut from 1½" strips to make 'Carrie Nation' block, dia. 7j. Putting several blocks together enables you to experiment with turning the blocks to give different directional designs, dia. 7k.

More than two strips

Now let's look at using more than two strips. It is best when stitching a number of strips together to alternate the direction in which you stitch, dia. 8. If you stitch all the strips the same way, especially if you haven't starched the fabric, it is possible to stretch the strips into a slight curve so that you end up with a banana-shaped strip-set instead of a rectangle.

dia. 8 Alternate stitch direction

If we stick with just two colours, but cut three 2½" strips of each and join them into two sets as shown, dia. 9a, we can make Basketweave and the 9-patch block in a similar way to the 4-patch we made earlier. Both of these blocks are great "mixers" and are most useful for setting together with more complex blocks.

dia. 9 Basketweave

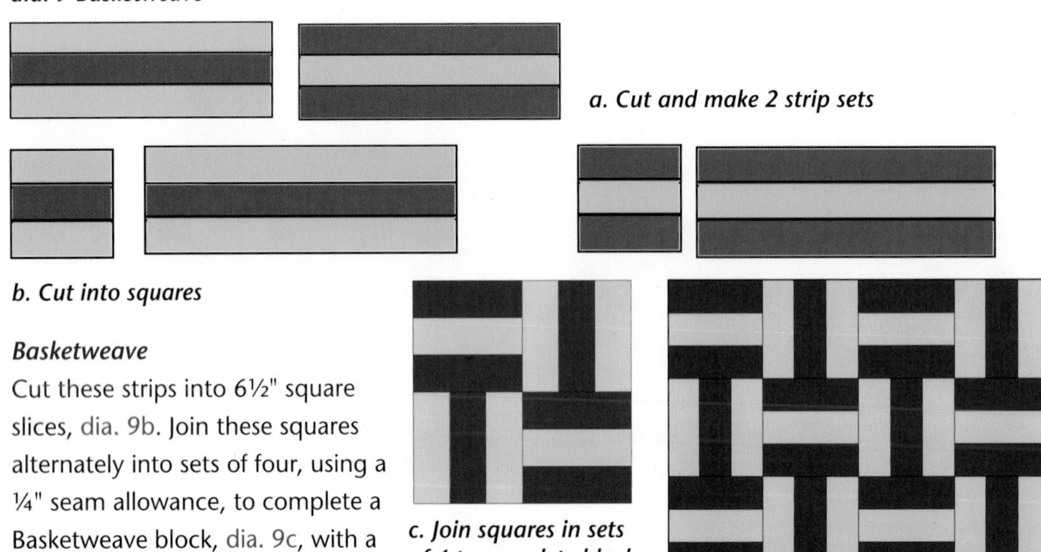

a. Cut and make 2 strip sets

b. Cut into squares

Basketweave

Cut these strips into 6½" square slices, dia. 9b. Join these squares alternately into sets of four, using a ¼" seam allowance, to complete a Basketweave block, dia. 9c, with a finished size of 12".

Four blocks put together show the "weave" to greater effect, dia. 9d.

Again, this is a good test of accuracy in measuring and cutting and in getting the seam allowance exact each time.

c. Join squares in sets of 4 to complete block

d. Four blocks put together

9-patch and Double 9-Patch

We can make 9-patch units by starting in exactly the same way, making two sets of strips from 2½" strips in two colours, dia. 10a. Use a ¼" seam allowance and press towards the darker fabric each time so that you match the seams when you sew the slices together.

Cut 2½" slices from these sets, two from one set and one from the second, and rejoin to make a 9-patch unit, dia. 10b.

dia. 10. 9-patch

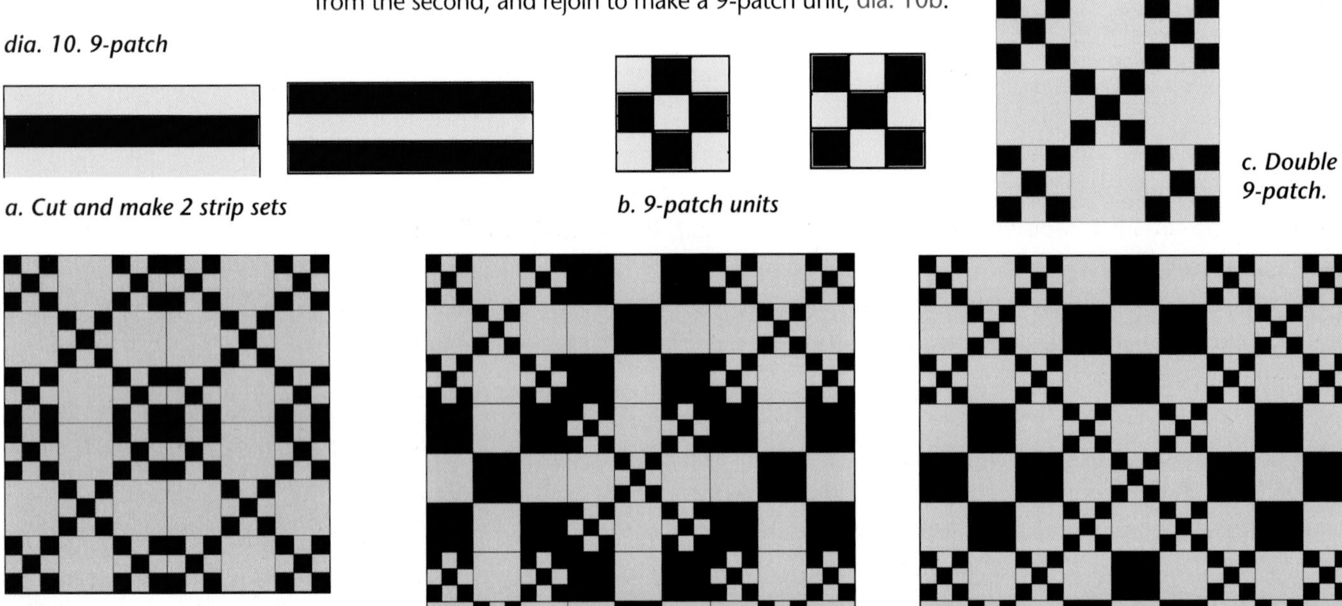

a. Cut and make 2 strip sets

b. 9-patch units

c. Double 9-patch.

d. 4 Double 9-patch blocks

e. Single 9-patch and Double 9-Patch blocks put together.

A Double 9-patch has a plain square alternating with a 9-patch unit, dia. 10c. Cut the plain square 6½".
These measurements will make a finished size block of 18" (3 x 6).

Starting with narrower strips will make a smaller block – strips cut to 1½" for example will make 3" 9-patch blocks (which, with 3½" plain squares between, will make a 9" (3 x 3) Double 9-patch), or 6" Basketweave blocks.

Stretched 9-Patch
This is another useful block made from three strips of two colours (although you can use more if you wish). This time however the strips are different widths to start with.

Cut 2, 2½" strips and 1, 4½" strip in each of your two colours. Stitch them together into two strip sets, dia. 11a. From one strip set cut 2, 2½" slices and from the other cut 1, 4½" slice, dia. 11b. Stitch these three slices together to complete the block, dia. 11c.

Try using a big print for the squares (pink), or a mixture of prints for these while keeping the rectangles plain. Look what happens when you put several together, dia. 11d.

dia. 11 Stretched 9-Patch

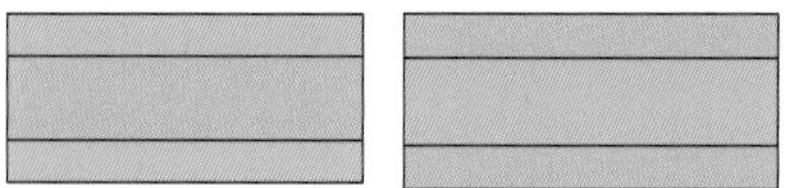

a. Cut and make 2 strip sets

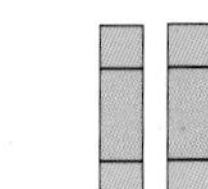
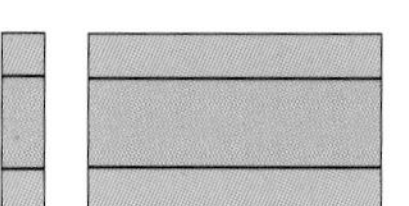

b. Cut into segments

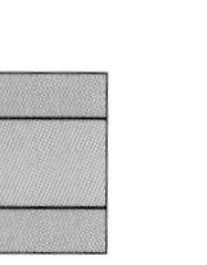
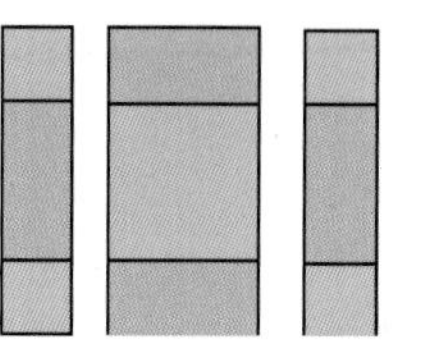
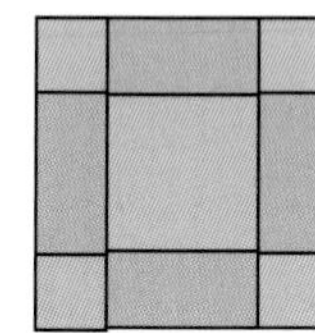

c. Stitch together to complete block

d. 9 blocks put together

Rail Fence and Windmill
Rail Fence is another popular block which is easy to make from strip-sets.
Cut 4, 2" strips in different colours – you can grade them light to dark as shown if you wish.

Join the four strips, pressing the seams to the darker fabric, dia. 12a. Cut 6½" squares from this strip set, dia. 12b. Join four squares together to make 12" finished size Rail Fence or Windmill blocks, dia, 12c and dia. 12d.

dia. 12 Rail Fence

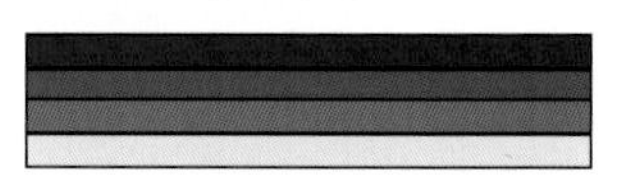

a. Join 4 strips

b. Cut squares

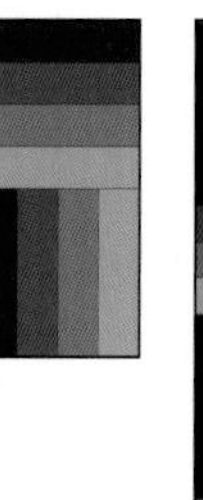

c. Rail Fence

d. Windmill

Experiment and have fun using different width strips. For example cut 1, 2½" strip and 1, 1½" strip, to see what designs you can make with those. Or play with the designs to see what you can make by using coloured paper in strips, cut them apart to play with – it's considerably cheaper than fabric, but far less satisfying!

Triangles and diamonds

We've already looked at strip piecing a variety of designs by just cutting squares and rectangles from stripped bands. Now let's look at designs you can make by cutting those bands into triangles or diamonds. (We would recommend once more that you starch your fabric before cutting as this helps to keep its shape and prevent fraying.)

Just two strips

Cutting triangles

Cut 1, 2½" strip from each of your two fabrics. Join them with ¼" seam, as before and press to the darker fabric, dia. 13a. Then cut 8, 4½" squares from the strip, dia. 13b. Now cut 4 of these squares diagonally one way and 4 the other way, dia. 13c. The first time through you may prefer to mark the diagonal lines with chalk or pencil before making the 45° cuts into triangles. If you are feeling confident then you could just use the 45° line on the ruler or mat and cut directly. You can rejoin these to make two versions of one of Chris's favourite blocks – Twilight, dia. 13d, and its reverse companion, dia. 13e.

dia. 13 Twilight

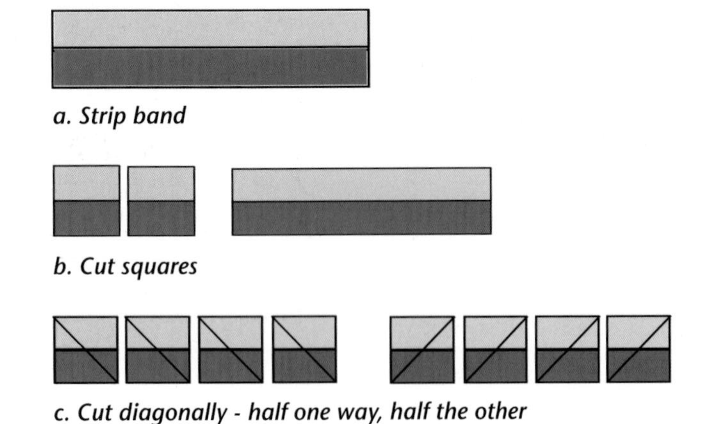

a. Strip band

b. Cut squares

c. Cut diagonally - half one way, half the other

d. Twilight...

e. ... and its reverse

If, however, you cut right angled triangles from the strip band as shown, dia. 14a, you can make this Four X Variation, dia. 14b. This is a block which is fast to make and has great 3D qualities. Compare this one with dia. 16.

dia. 14. Four X Variation

a. Cut right-angled triangles

b. Four X Variation

Cutting 60° triangles or diamonds

In the same way that cutting strips and joining them together before cutting squares and right angled triangles produces quick and interesting patterns, so too does cutting diamonds or 60° triangles from pieced strip sets.

As before, cut and stitch together 2, 2½" strips, pressing the seam to the darker fabric, dia. 15a. Cut 60° triangles, dia. 15b, or diamonds, dia. 15c, perpendicular to the long edge using the 60° line on your ruler. If you prefer, you can mark the cutting lines with chalk or pencil first. See what happens when you cut them parallel to the long edge, dia. 15d.

dia. 15 Cutting diamonds and triangles

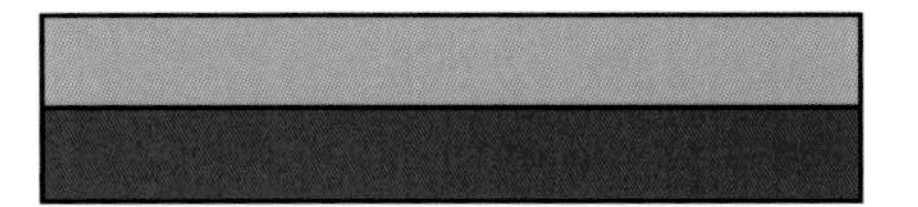

a. Strip band

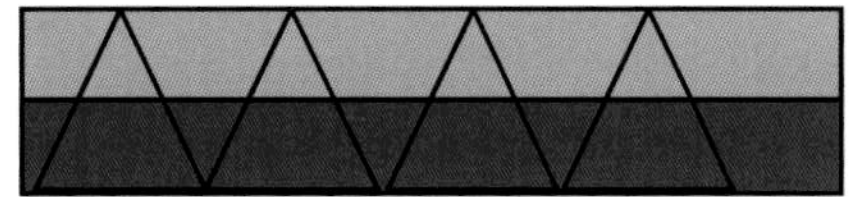

b. Cut 60° triangles

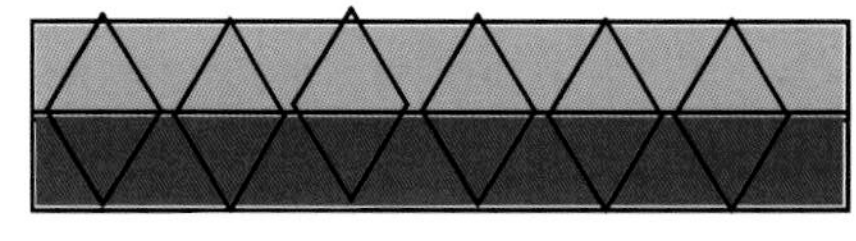

c. or diamonds

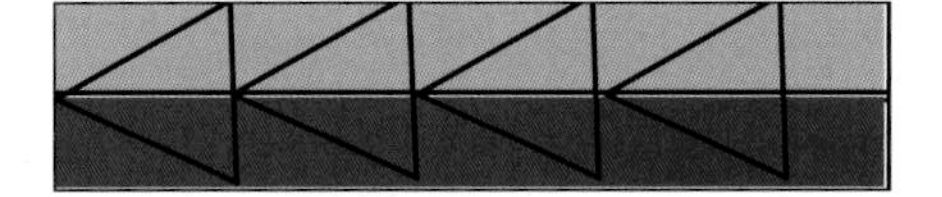

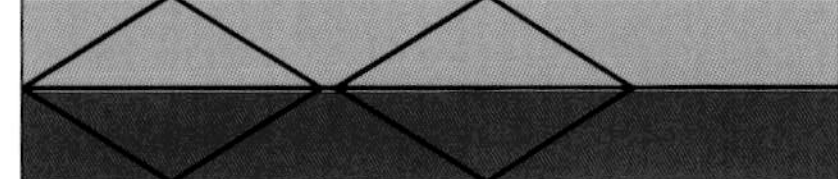

d. Cut parallel to long edge

e. Possibilities

Combine these shapes cut from strip bands with those cut from plain fabric. You can use the perpendicular triangles with plain triangles (or diamonds) to make Hollow Boxes and the diamonds will make interesting Eight-Pointed Stars, dia. 15e.

More than two strips

Now let's look at using more than two strips. Remember to alternate the direction in which you stitch, dia. 8. Again we can cut right-angles triangles from strip-sets with two, three or more colours.

Four X Variation

Cut 1½" strips and join them in sets of three as shown, dia. 16a, using two or three colours as preferred. Cut apart into right-angled triangles to make this Four X variation block, dia. 16b.

dia. 16 Four X Variation

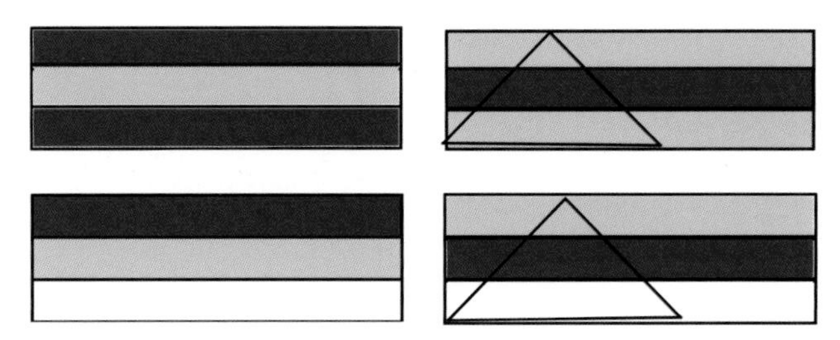

a. Strip bands; cut right-angled triangles

b. Four X variation block

Mock Half-Square Log Cabin

Now make a strip set using 1½" strips in at least five colours ranging from light to dark, dia. 17a. Cut squares and then slice these in half diagonally – half one way and half the other, dia. 17b. Rejoin to form squares, dia. 17c.

dia. 17 Mock Half-square Log Cabin

a. Strip band

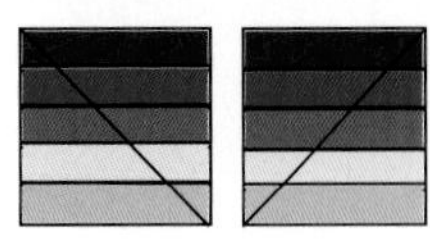

b. Cut squares diagonally

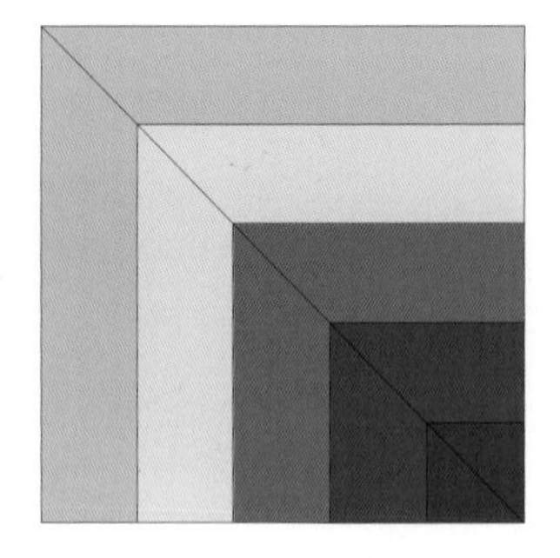

c. Rejoin

Roman Stripe

Make a stripped band in assorted colours using 4, 2" strips, dia. 18a. Cut 1 contrast 8½" strip. Place this, right sides together, with the stripped band and stitch along both long edges to make a tube, dia. 18b. Cut the tube into right-angled triangles, dia. 18c. Open out each triangle – you may have to snip a stitch or two at the point - and press carefully to complete the block, dia. 18d. Just be aware that this method means all the block sides are on the bias so handle with care, even if they have been starched until rigid.

dia. 18 Roman Stripe

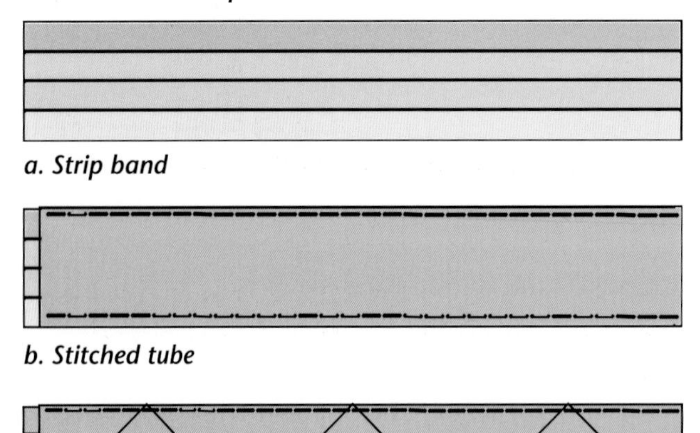

a. Strip band

b. Stitched tube

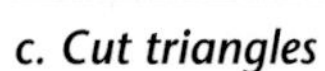

c. Cut triangles

d. Completed block

There are other ways of using strips for easy piecing that give complex results. To begin with you could try using different width strips, for example cut 1, 2½" strip and 1, 1½" strip and join them together and see what happens when you cut them into squares, triangles or diamonds. And, as we've suggested before, you could try ideas out using strips of paper rather than fabric before approaching your precious fabric stash. On the other hand, it is only fabric (which is meant to be used) and you will hardly notice one or two 2½" strips taken from some of your favourites.

Sashings, settings and borders

Congratulations! You've made the blocks and you're all set to join them together and complete the quilt top. This is the stage we think is the most fun of all – looking at lots of possibilities and easy-but-different ways to put blocks together, playing with the placement and moving things around. Both of us can produce various piles of blocks that haven't been put together yet because we've had so much fun trying to decide which setting will look the best. We're going to use our dependable and favourite Sawtooth Star block, dia. 1, to illustrate just a few of the basic setting and border options you might like to explore before taking your blocks to the sewing machine.

dia. 1 Sawtooth Star block

Sashings and settings

Edge to edge

An edge to edge setting is the most basic with blocks just stitched together to make the quilt top, dia. 2a. This works well if you have cut and stitched accurately throughout and all the blocks are exactly the same size. For most of us this is perhaps more easily said than done and that is probably one of the good reasons for using a simple setting that helps overcome and disguise any small discrepancies in block size.

A fast and easy way to make your blocks stretch twice as far is to alternate them with a plain or simply pieced block – almost twice the area for the same amount of work! Of course it takes more fabric but then this could be an excellent excuse to go in search of just the right fabric to enhance your blocks or you could forage through your stash. A very simple pieced block, such as Hour Glass or Square in a Square, can look most effective, dia. 2b, and is a good way of using several fabrics which can make a more interesting quilt.

dia. 2 Edge to edge settings

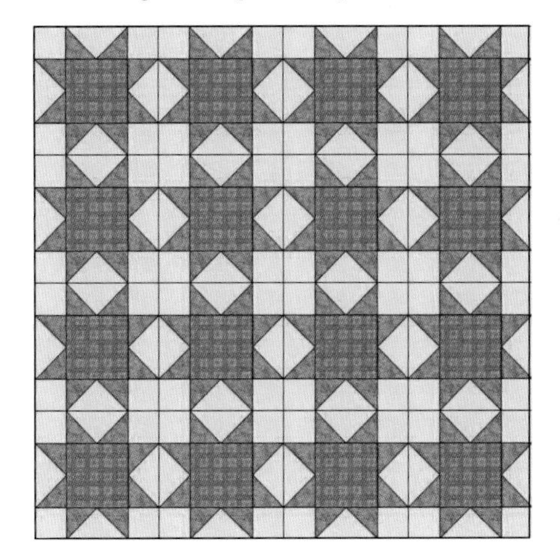

a. Same block side by side

b. Alternate with a simple block

c. Blocks set on point

One setting option that we think is almost always worth exploring is to set the blocks on point – it really is surprising what a difference this makes as you can see from dia. 2c. Also, blocks set on point occupy more space than blocks set straight – Chris usually mutters that it's something to do with Pythagoras – which we think is another bonus. On a practical note you will want to consider grain line when cutting the setting triangles that complete the quilt and have the straight grain running along the long edge.

Setting triangles for blocks on point

The magic number to remember is 1.414.

Side setting triangles

For these edge or side triangles, to get the straight grain running down the sides we need to cut quarter-square triangles, i.e. 4 are cut from a square, dia. A. To get the correct size of square from which to cut these triangles, **multiply** by 1.414.

Example – the finished size of the block is 8"; multiply by 1.414 (= 11.312); add the seam allowance (1¼" for quarter square triangles); round up the answer to the nearest ⅛.

(8 x 1.414) + 1.25 = 12.562 = 12⅝ when rounded up.

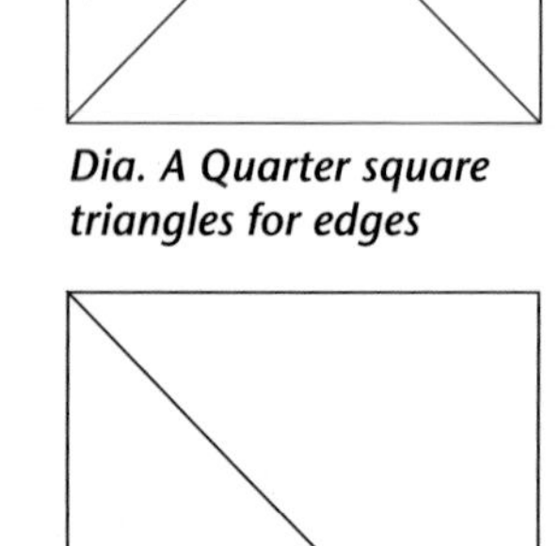

Dia. A Quarter square triangles for edges

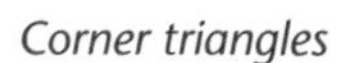

Corner triangles

For corner triangles we need to cut half-square triangles, dia. B, to get the corners on the straight grain. To get the correct size of square from which to cut these triangles, **divide** by 1.414.

Example – the finished size of the block is 8"; divide by 1.414; add the seam allowance (⅞" for half-square triangles); round up the answer to the nearest ⅛.

(8 / 1.414) + ⅞" = 5.677 + 0.875 = 6.5327 = 6⅝" rounded up.

Dia. B Half-square triangles for corners

Sashing

Sashing is the term for joining blocks with strips and it has some serious advantages – it frames the blocks and minimises those infuriating discrepancies in size, and it makes the quilt top bigger with very little extra work. Sashings can be plain or fancy, simple strips of fabric or stripped, pieced and complex. We've shown plain sashing, dia. 3a, sashing with setting squares, dia. 3b, and stripped sashing, dia. 3c. The same three settings but turned on point are shown in dia. 4.

dia. 3 Sashed straight settings

a. Plain sashing

b. Sashing with setting squares

c. Strip-pieced sashing

dia. 4 Sashed on-point settings

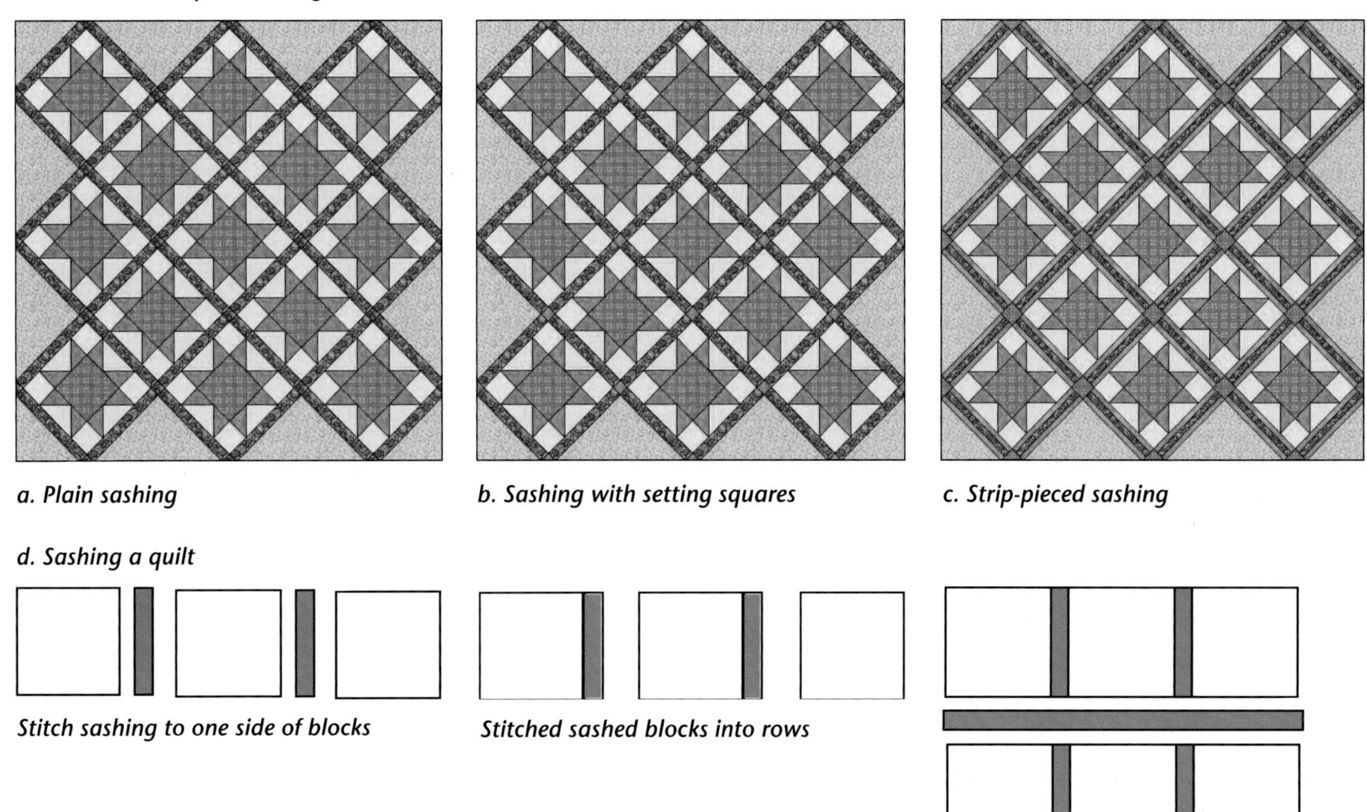

a. Plain sashing

b. Sashing with setting squares

c. Strip-pieced sashing

d. Sashing a quilt

Stitch sashing to one side of blocks

Stitched sashed blocks into rows

Stitch sashing between rows

Sashing comes into its own with sampler quilts, or if you want to make a quilt using a number of different blocks. Just setting the blocks edge to edge, unless you have chosen blocks and planned carefully for this, results in each block losing its identity and the whole design becoming a mish-mash, dia. 5a. The sashing, whether simple or more complex, allows each block to retain its integrity and stand alone within its sashing frame, dia. 5b.

dia. 5 Sampler quilts

a. Straight sets can lose identity

b. Sashing keeps integrity of blocks

Increasing block size

What about setting your blocks by making them a little bit bigger with some simple piecing? This is another way of disguising those sneaky differences in block sizes – Chris's favourite is the Twist and Turn, dia. 6.

Trim block around square to create 'twist and turn'

dia. 6 'Twist and Turn' setting to enlarge blocks

Add strips around your square – use strips that are a minimum of 2½" deep.

Then place a square ruler (or template) over the new square at a random angle – the sharper the angle, the more twist you will get in your block.

If you want to add a lot of twist you will need to have wider strips than if you only want a slight twist.

Grouping

What happens if you group your blocks? You could put blocks together in sets of four to make new bigger blocks as shown in dia. 7. The new bigger blocks could then be set straight or on point, edge to edge or sashed, and so on…

Grouping your blocks into strips and then following a strippy format is another possibility, dia. 8.

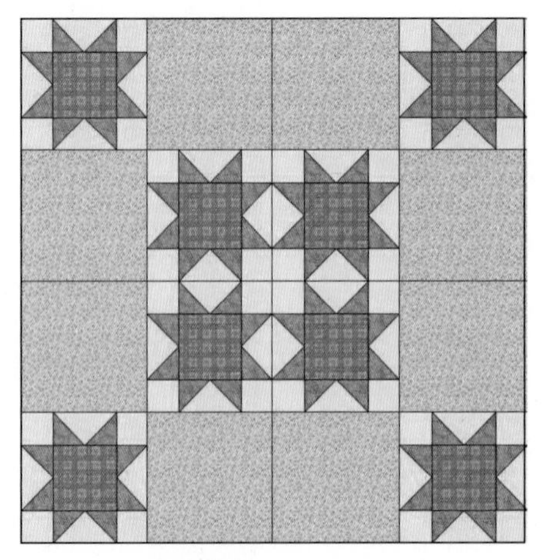

dia. 7. Grouped blocks

dia. 8. Strippy setting

Some practicalities

Setting your blocks with sashings is simple and straightforward, especially if you plan ahead. Measure and cut your strips as accurately as you can, preferably from selvedge to selvedge of the fabric to minimise distortion of the strips. We like to have both the blocks and the sashing fabrics starched to within an inch of their lives, which we think helps handling. Make a sketch plan showing the rows of blocks and sashings or, if you have room, lay the blocks out on the floor or a design wall. Work systematically along each row adding a sashing strip to the left side of each block, and a strip on both left and right of the end block. Next, stitch a strip to the lower edge of each block. Join the row into a single length. (Alternatively, you could join the blocks together and then add a long strip of sashing to the lower edge). Press the seams carefully, either open or to one side, but not a mixture of both. You may find that pressing the seam allowance toward the sashings works well.

Join the lengths of blocks into pairs – take time with plenty of pins and everything lined up and stitch slowly, with your work supported rather than pulling and dragging over the edge of the machine and the table. Then, again taking time and those well-used pins, join the paired lengths together until the quilt top is complete and can be given a celebratory pressing.

Borders

Borders are probably the most neglected area of the quilt – they don't always have to be elaborate but we think that they do merit some time and consideration. It really is like framing a picture in terms of the final effect and can make a huge amount of difference to the finished piece. We'll start off with the visual aspect of borders and then look into some of the practicalities of construction.

Way back when dinosaurs walked the earth and we were just starting out in patchwork the standard practice was to make lots of blocks, join them together perhaps with some daring sashing (!) and then finish everything off with wide strips of a vaguely appropriate fabric to make the border. This basic approach is still valid and is far better than no border at all. If you do decide on one simple border to finish the quilt it's a good idea to try out several fabrics for effect before making your choice – you can see from dia. 9 just how different the same quilt looks with a light fabric border and dark fabric border. Sometimes introducing a new colour for the border works

dia. 9. Colour value

a. Light border

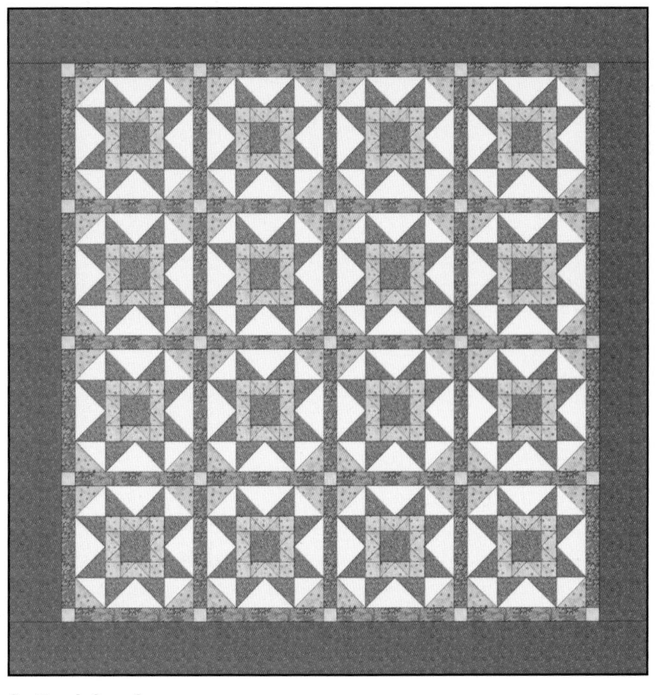

b. Dark border

dia. 10. Introduce a new colour

a. Plain

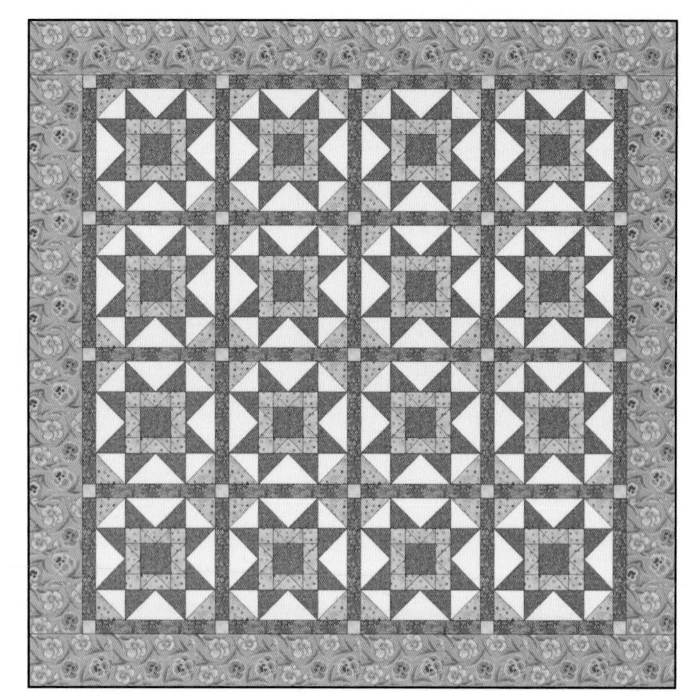

b. Multiprint

well, and at other times you may prefer to use the border as an opportunity to collect up some of the colours already used in the quilt blocks, dia. 10. (Many of us spend lots of time searching for just the right fabric to use for a border – you've probably seen us in your local quilt shop or at quilt shows, clutching a few odd scraps of fabric and wearing a grim, determined expression..............)

dia. 11. Pieced strips or leftovers

If you can't find the perfect border fabric, or if you don't have quite enough of it, you might want to consider using leftovers from the blocks to piece together as shown in dia. 11. Adding in squares at the corners and centres of the border strips is a great way of making the best of "not quite enough" fabric – by adding fabric in a balanced and symmetrical fashion no-one will ever know that this is really a Plan B solution.

dia. 12 Different width borders

a. 2"

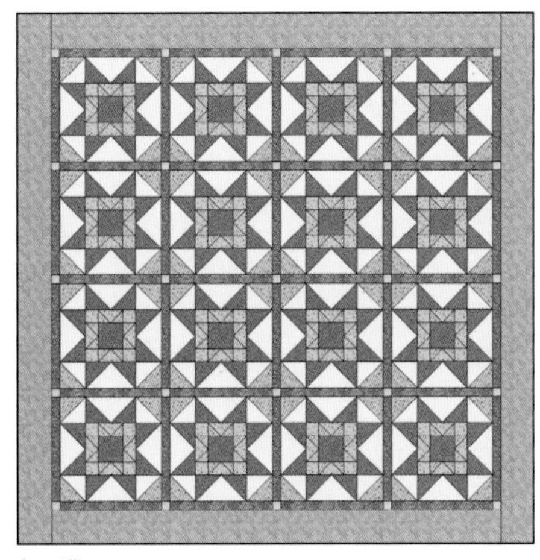

b. 6"

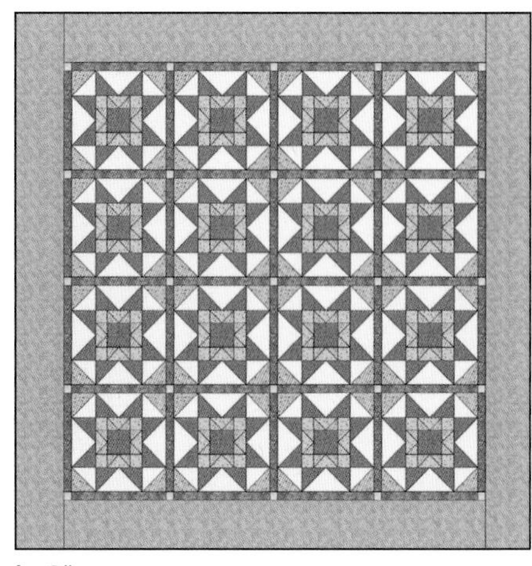

b. 8"

With regard to the thorny question of how wide/deep a border should be a very general rule of thumb is to have the border no less than a third and no more than half the width of the blocks. So if the blocks were 12", the final border could be between 4" and 6". If you look at the quilts shown in dia. 12 you can get an idea of how this works – the borders shown are proportionally 2", 6" and 8" on the same quilt of 12" blocks.

As an aside we'd just like to mention that, when we're following a project in a book or magazine, we prefer to measure and cut our borders to fit the quilt after, repeat after, we've put all the blocks together. Many quilt "recipes" give precise measurements for border strips and, if you cut precious fabric to these exact measurements before you begin you may just find that your piecing and pre-cut borders don't match up. Cue for much unhappiness and the discovery that there is no more of that particular fabric to be found anywhere on the planet.

There are a number of easy border options which can add pizazz, emphasis and all sorts of exciting things to your quilt top. On several occasions we have opted for a "piano key" border made up of strips pieced together randomly then cut and rejoined into border lengths – this is not only quick and easy but very effective as well, dia. 13. It is surprising how often two borders, an inner narrow one and an outer, wider one give a more satisfactory finish to a quilt than a single border. Perhaps this is because the inner, narrow border is an opportunity to pick up one of the accent colours from the quilt, or perhaps there is no reason at all, sometimes it just looks better! Judge for yourself with dia. 14.

Alternatively you could join longer strips into bands of border length. From this point it is a short step to considering some simple cutting and re-arranging for a different look, dia. 15.

dia. 13 Piano key stripped border

dia. 14 Several borders

dia. 15. Rail Fence border

dia. 16. Triangle and diamond borders

a. Triangles

b. Diamonds

What about using some easy shapes to make a pieced border? – you could experiment with squares, triangles, 60° triangles, or diamonds, dia. 16.

Practicalities

In a perfect world all quilt borders would be straight and true – no unsightly ripples or slightly curved seams. To achieve your goal it's worth slowing down your working pace and curbing your enthusiasm (and need) to get the quilt top finished. Spend some time pressing the quilt top and trimming loose or long threads so that everything is as tidy as possible before you begin.

Decide on the width of your border strips and measure the quilt top carefully to determine the length required – this is best done by measuring across and then down the centre of the quilt rather than along the edges.

If you want to have a border with butted corners, dia. 17a, you might want to stitch the two side border strips first followed by the top and bottom strips – this keeps things balanced and in better shape than working your way around the quilt top in rotation. Butted corners are often used because they're fast and easy. Whilst this is true we've seen plenty of butted corners that are not entirely square to the quilt so, again, do take time to be as accurate as possible during the stitching. Pin, pin and pin again is the motto here!

dia. 17 Corners

a. Butted

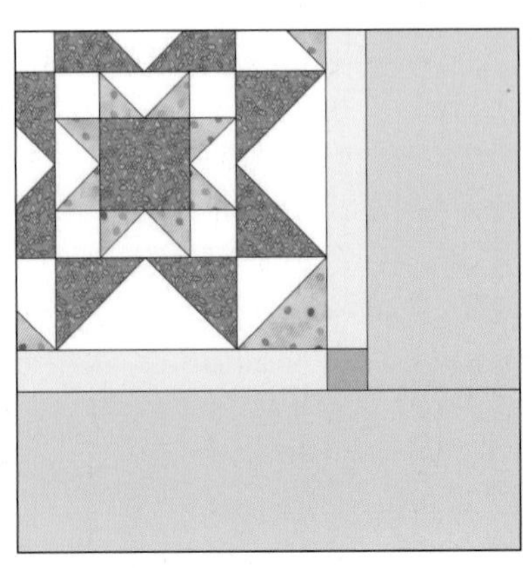

Detail of butted corner

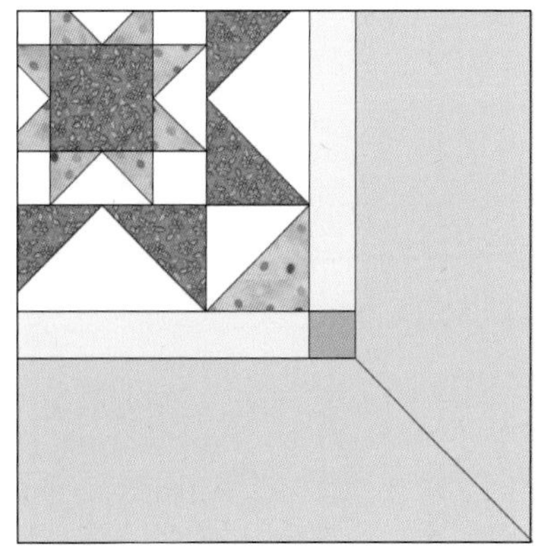

Detail of mitred corner

TIP

It is not considered good practice to mix mitred and butted corners on the same quilt – and it looks vaguely unsatisfactory too!

b. Mitred

Mitred corners, dia. 17b, look good and are a lot easier to do than you might think, they just need care with measuring and steady accurate stitching. Mitreing requires plenty of fabric rather than trying to squeeze borders out of restricted yardage. Over the years we've seen various suggestions for how to mitre and the method that we've used most often is one we think was suggested by well-known US quilt designer Judy Martin back in the 1980s. We've shown the steps with photographs, photos1a - h, using an orphan block rather than a whole quilt – and we think it's a good idea to use a spare block to see how it works for yourself. Each border strip needs to be the required length plus twice the width of the strip with a little extra added in for seams.

So for instance on a 12" quilt/block with a 3" border your border strips would need to be 12" plus 6" which would be 18" plus extra for seams and reassurance – we'd say 20" for the total strip length required.

- Position, pin and stitch all 4 border strips in place, beginning and finishing each seam a measured and marked ¼" from the outside edge, photos 1a - c.
- Fold back the 2 side border strips so that the RS is facing you. Leave the top and bottom strips unturned with WS facing you.
- With a ruler and fabric marker draw the 45° line to connect the stopped line of stitch and the point where the two strips overlap, photo 1d.
- Mark this line at all four corners.
- Fold the quilt top diagonally so that the two border strips are aligned, photo 1e, (pin either side of the marked line for extra peace of mind) and then stitch on the marked line, beginning at the ¼" point.
- Stitch all four corners in the same way and check each one carefully before trimming away to a ¼" seam allowance, photos 1f - g.
- This seam allowance can be pressed open and the long joining seams will also benefit from pressing at this stage, photo 10h.

Photo 1. Mitred Border

a. Border strip pinned in place

b. Stitched ¼" from outside edge

c. Next border strip in position ready for stitching

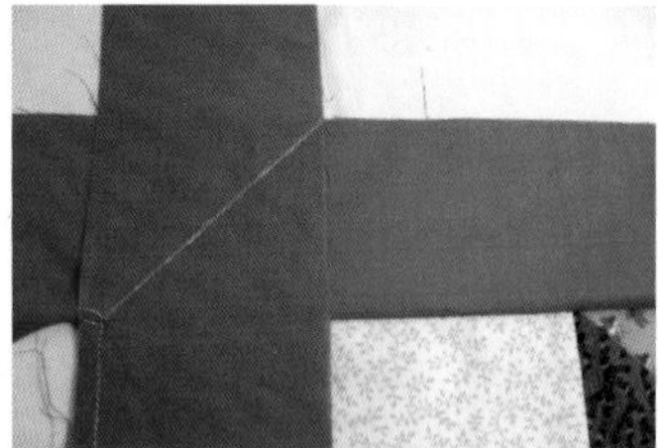

d. Strips overlapped with stitching line marked

e. Border strips aligned, quilt folded on diagonal

f. Check the mitre before trimming

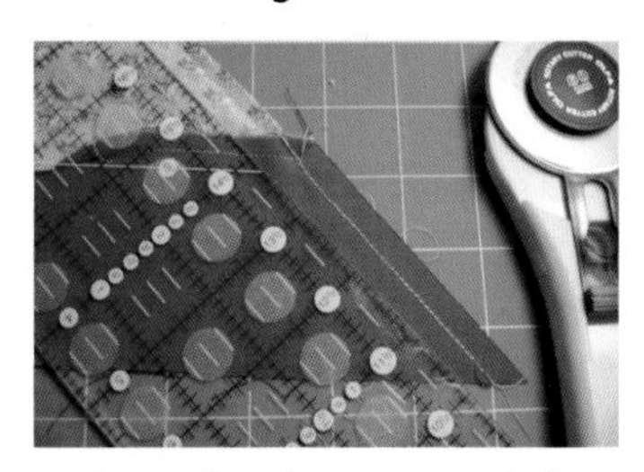

g. Carefully trim away to ¼" seam allowance

h. The finished mitred corner

Quilting

Once upon a time in the days before the arrival of Mr Singer's amazing patented machine (circa 1860) all quilting was done by hand. Nowadays we can choose to quilt either by hand or machine – two separate and distinct skills, both equally valid and correct and both techniques can be combined in one project.

General preparation

Press the whole top taking care to trim any remaining threads and make sure that all the seams are pressed according to your preference.
For machine quilting starching the top and back will give the quilt a bit of body to help prevent those terrible twins 'creep' and 'pucker'; it will also give some extra 'slip and slide' to help the quilt move under the machine.

Markers and marking the design

Just talking about the many different markers and marking methods could take up several pages – we sometimes get a little overwhelmed ourselves with all the choices and possibilities! Stating the downright obvious we reckon you'll need a pale-coloured marker to use on dark fabrics and another, different coloured marker for pale fabrics. Always test your chosen marker on scraps of fabric first to make sure that it is visible and can be removed when the stitching is complete. Mark lightly and be prepared to refresh these markings as the work progresses. Avoid the temptation to mark so heavily that the design will be clearly visible across the room and throughout the stitching time. Remember, this is not rocket science but more common sense! Heavy marking is usually impossible/very difficult to remove at a later stage and can really spoil the final effect. And there is no point in using a water-soluble marker on fabric that cannot be thoroughly wetted once the project is complete.

TIP

Here are three of our top tips:

- curved lines of quilting often look good with the straight lines of piecing
- straight lines of quilting often look good with the curved lines of applique
- outline quilting looks good in most situations and is a great start

Where do you get your patterns from?

This is one of the big questions for both machine and hand quilters. You can use all sorts of interesting things like stencils, templates, freehand drawing, rulers to make designs. Often in project instructions you will find the dreaded phrase "quilt as desired" which many of us find hugely unhelpful! If you have no idea what to quilt where, and therefore what patterns you could choose, we recommend you study pictures of quilts in magazines, books and shows to see what you think looks good. The best advice we can give you is to keep it simple and straightforward.

In photos 1 and 2 you can see circles of hand quilting worked on strip-piecing and straight(ish) lines of quilting following the seams and shapes of the pieced design.

You can buy stencils and printed patterns specially for machine quilting – they don't have too many stops and starts – look for ones that say 'continuous line' patterns.
Or you can draw your own – use plates and cups for circles and arcs, photo 3, practice the gentle art of doodling by machine (also known as 'meander quilting' or sometimes 'vermicelli'), or just follow some of the designs on your printed fabrics.

Marking the design

Transferring a design to the fabric can seem to be fraught with danger and difficulty. In fact it's nowhere near as mysterious as you might think and largely dependent on what design you have chosen.

Most marking strategies are best undertaken before the layers are put together. Quilting in the ditch, which is stitching along the seam lines of the patchwork, requires no marking – just follow the seam lines.

If you want to quilt anywhere else you need to mark either the full line or the target spots to hit with your machine stitching, photos 4a and b.

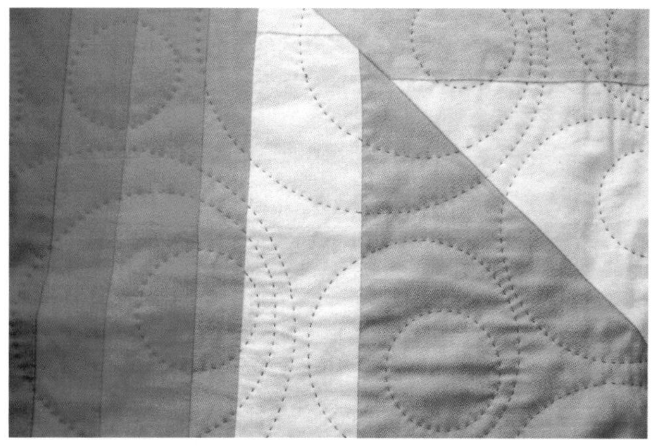

1. Circles quilted on a stripped piece

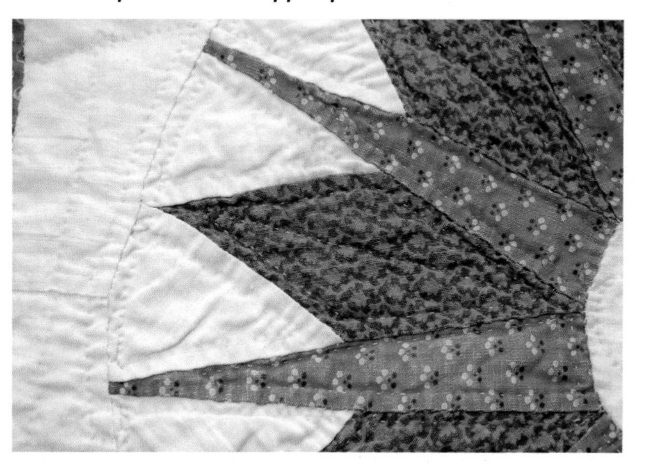

2. Straight lines and outlines

3. Use everyday objects to make quilting designs

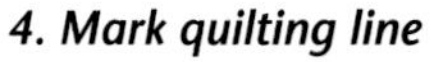

4. Mark quilting line

a. Marked line

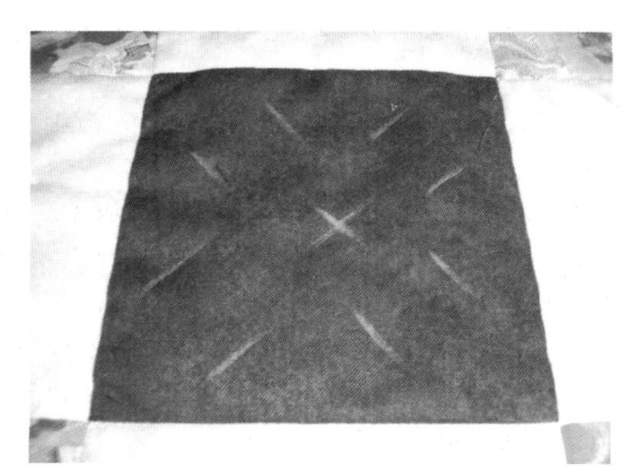

b. Marked targets

Machine quilters can also use paper patterns on top of the quilt, photo 5. The quilt is not marked and the paper is torn away afterwards. You can buy special quilters paper, or tracing paper, greaseproof paper, something that is see-through, stitch-through and tearable. You can also now buy wash-away stabiliser paper which works quite well. Again, try them and see which one works for you.

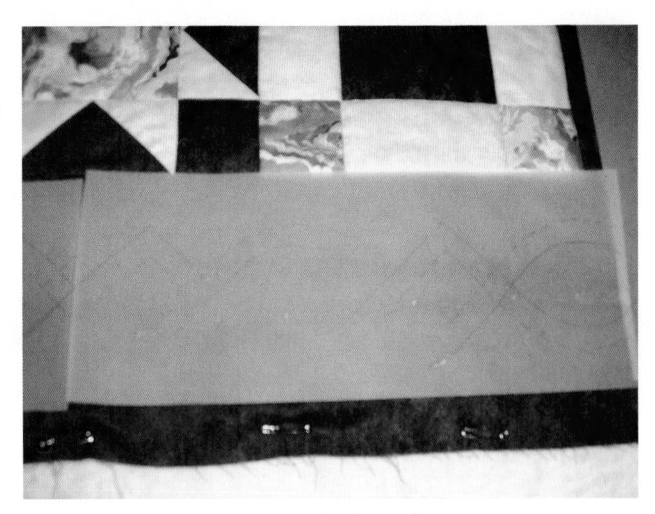

5. Using tracing paper to quilt through

Draw the design on the paper, spray baste or pin it into position, stitch through and tear away.

Choosing the wadding and backing

This is an area of many choices, labels and different fibres and lots of potential confusion. There is no one "right" batting but for hand quilting we think it's a good idea to start with a lightweight cotton/polyester mix or an all-polyester batting. Needlepunched battings are great for machine quilting as they cling to your top and backing and reduce a lot of the creep that can occur when stitching. However these battings are not always the easiest to hand quilt, particularly if you want to make small stitches with ease. Thicker, loftier batting is not necessarily a good choice in terms of easy stitching – Barbara's first experience of hand quilting involved three layers of a very substantial 4oz batting which was most definitely not a good idea! Try different types of batting to see which one suits you and your particular project – some quilt shops offer sample packs at a small cost .

If you buy batting that has been rolled up in a package we recommend that you open it right out and lay it flat(tish) for a few hours or overnight before use. If time is really short you could lay the batting out and wave a hairdryer over it to get rid of the worst creases, or you could put it in a laundry dryer for a few turns.

Your backing fabric should be a similar weight to the top fabrics. If you don't want your first machine quilting efforts to show on the back, use a busy patterned fabric. Try not to economise by using polycotton sheeting as you may well be disappointed with the results. You can buy extra wide fabric for use as backing, or you can choose to piece your backing when making a very large bed quilt.

Preparing the layers

Press the backing fabric paying particular attention to any seams. We prefer to press these seams open rather than to one side because we think it is less intrusive and gives a flatter finish. Layer the backing, batting and quilt top together so that everything is as smooth and unwrinkled as possible. These layers need to be kept smooth and together while you are quilting which means that you need to do some form of tacking – and lots of it! This is the part of preparation that everyone professes to hate – yes, it's tedious, yes, it takes time but it really is necessary and so it's worth doing well.

For hand quilting you can tack the layers together, but for machine quilting you need to use other methods as the tacking stitches get caught in the machine. Chris usually spreads everything out on her tiled kitchen floor or old table and then uses masking tape to keep the layers smooth

6. *Tape the backing taut*

7. *Make a quilt sandwich*

dia. 1. Tacking

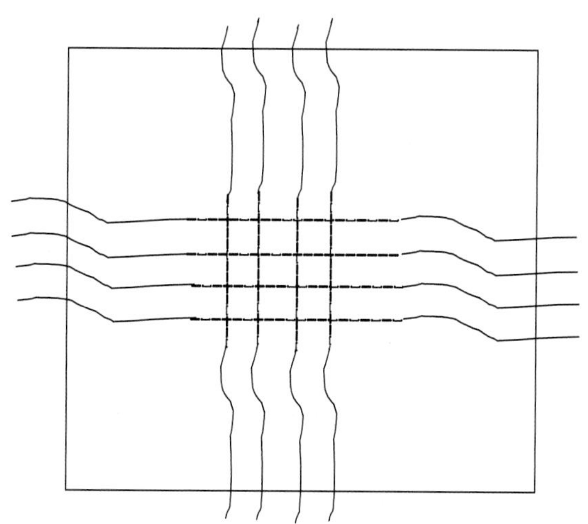

and taut photos 6 and 7 while she does the pinning for machine quilting. Or you could try Barbara's preferred method for hand quilting which centres the three layers on the kitchen table and tack the centre portion leaving long trailing threads, dia. 1. Once the entire centre is tacked in both directions with lines of large straight stitches about 3inches apart you can shift the tacked area to move on to the outer edges and continue the lines of tacking.

For machine quilting pin as closely as you would tack for hand quilting – in other words if you put your fist on the quilt you should have pins or tacking stitches touching each side.

Start at the middle, or at one corner, and fasten the layers together, smoothing as you go; it is best to quilt in this way too as then any fullness in the fabric will be eased to unquilted areas, dia. 2. For machine quilting you can use safety pins – special quilting ones, not nappy pins – or quilting tacks with a special gun, or spray baste. Chris prefers safety pins and Barbara the tacks for larger quilts while we both like the ease of spray basting for smaller pieces. While we would recommend the use of the tacking gun for hand quilting, the spray baste is not really suitable as it can gum up the needle and making stitching difficult.

dia. 2. Stitching direction

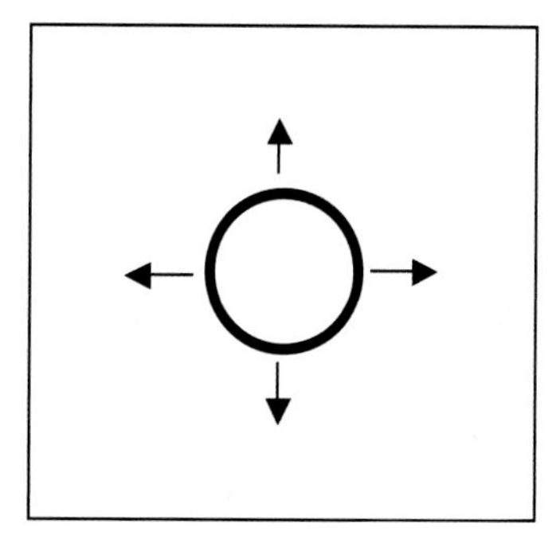

a. from centre

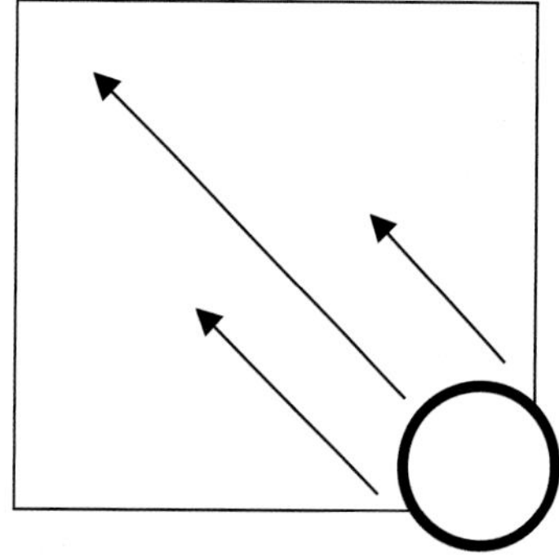

b. from corner

If you are concerned about fitting a large king-size quilt under the sewing machine try the popular divide and conquer strategy. Split the wadding into three (or more) equal strips, sandwich the centre portion only, baste and then quilt that first. Add one of the outside pieces – make sure the wadding strips butt up to each other well without major overlaps or gaps, roughly tack them together and then baste and quilt that section. Repeat with the remaining third.

Machine quilting

There are two main types of machine to quilt with – we're talking about quilting using a home sewing machine, not a commercially sized long-arm machine. With the feed dogs up and a regular or "walking" machine foot in place you can stitch straight lines and gentle curves. Drop the feed dogs and use a darning foot to do 'free-machine' or 'free-motion' quilting, where you are responsible for moving the fabric under the needle.

What machine do I need?

You can machine quilt on pretty much any machine so long as it makes a straight stitch and goes forwards. It's a lot easier if the machine is electrically powered because that way you have both hands free. Some machines have a built in even-feed system which is great for coping with the extra thickness of the three layers. We think a walking foot is an excellent investment – a walking foot helps all the layers to feed evenly through under the needle. We often use a walking foot for stitching on quilt borders or putting rows of blocks together as well as quilting. An open-toed darning foot will also be useful if you want to do free motion quilting. Photo 8 shows an ordinary machine foot, a walking foot, and two types of open-toe darning foot, the larger one designed specifically for free-motion quilting. Some modern machines now have a speed limiter – which is a bit like cruise control on a car – you set a comfortable (legal?) speed, take your foot off the pedal and the machine does the rest. This is great for free-machining as keeping the speed even while keeping the fabric moving evenly can be like patting your head and rubbing your stomach.

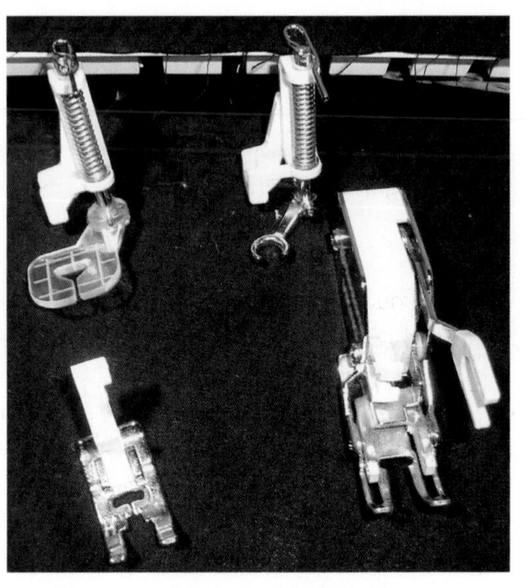

8. Different machine feet for quilting

What threads do you use?

Another thorny question. The bobbin thread should be reasonably fine; it can match the backing if you don't want it to show on the back, or it can match the top thread if you fear your tension may not be working too well and you don't want 'dots' of thread appearing on the top. There is at least one new thread currently available designed specifically for use in the bobbin when machine quilting.

The number of threads available for use on the top is mind-boggling, photo 9. The first decision is - how much do you want your quilting to show? If the answer is 'not at all', then consider using either an invisible quilting

9. A few of the machine threads available

thread (monofilament) or a thread that most closely matches the top. Otherwise you can find variegated threads in a wide range of colours, metallic threads or rayon threads to add glitter or a bit of a sheen to your stitching, or you can use thicker embroidery threads. These threads take a little understanding and adjustment to use them successfully in your machine. Metallic and similar threads may require a needle with a larger eye, such as a topstitch needle, to prevent them fraying and breaking. Thicker embroidery threads often work best if used in the bobbin and the piece is quilted from the wrong side. As every machine is different, experiment with your machine to see what it enjoys doing and what it is capable of doing.

To start off, try using monofilament thread on the top and 50s or 60s count thread in bobbin with a walking/even-feed foot to quilt all the basic construction (seam) lines. This will hold the layers together and you may decide that the quilt doesn't require any more quilting than that. If it does need more quilting – in the borders, say, or setting squares – you will perhaps have a better idea of what to do once this basic quilting is complete, photo 10.

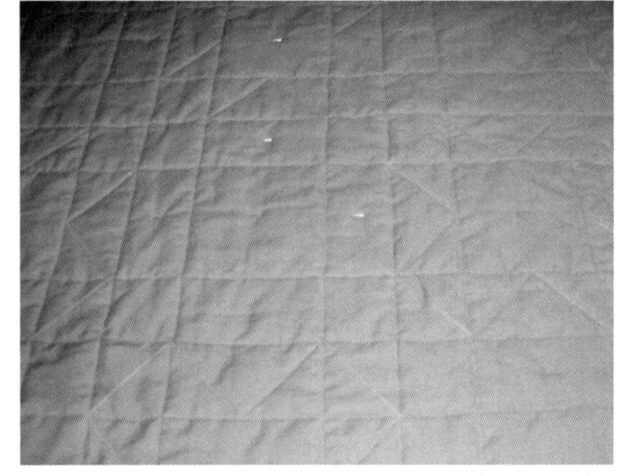

10. Construction lines quilted

Needles

Change your needle often, after about 8 hours of sewing. Check your machine handbook for suggestions of thread/needle size combinations. You will often find that a metallic thread will stitch better if fed through a topstitch needle. You can also buy 'quilting' machine needles and 'metallic thread' needles. Again, try them to see which work best for you and your machine. The most important thing though is to buy good quality needles – don't be tempted by cheap ones.

Setting up the machine

Make up a trial quilt sandwich using the same (or similar weight) fabrics and wadding as for your quilt. This trial piece is used to set your machine up with the correct tension, foot pressure and stitch length for the quilting you will be doing. Thread the machine with the same types of thread you will be using, but make sure the bobbin and top threads are different colours and contrast well with the trial piece.

The stitch for machine quilting is (usually) your normal straight stitch set to, perhaps, a slightly longer stitch length than for piecing; so set this first and then do a trial length of stitches. Look carefully at how the stitches lie in the fabric, dia 3a -c. If the bobbin thread is showing through to the front you will need to either slacken the top tension or tighten the bottom. On the other hand, if the top thread comes through to the back you will need to do the opposite. Check your machine handbook to find out how to do this for your make of machine – they are all different. Once you've adjusted this, try doing a few gentle curves to make sure the tension behaves itself on these – sometimes the thread can pull into loops onto the back.

dia. 3. Setting the tension

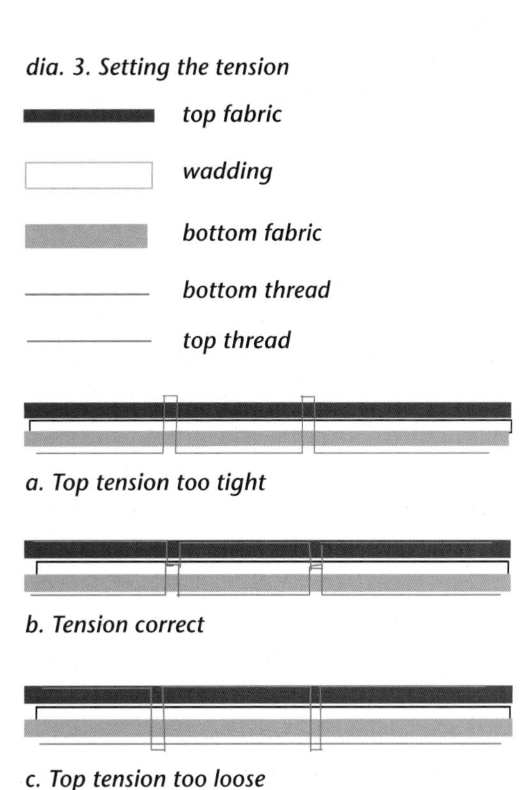

Once again make slight adjustments to the tension to counteract this; and try not to do very tight curves – keep them gentle.

Now do some lines of stitch at right angles to, and across, your first stitched lines. Are you getting puckers and tucks on the top or the bottom? Tucks on the top are often because the fabric is creeping under the foot. Are you able to adjust the pressure on the foot? Check your handbook and, if you can, slacken the pressure on the foot so it doesn't push so hard on the fabric. This is where a walking foot is so useful. Tucks and creep on the back usually mean that you didn't manage to stretch the backing taut enough or secure it sufficiently to stop it from shifting. Make sure you have used plenty of pins and that the backing fabric is nice and taut. Does the 'quilt' slide easily under the foot, especially for free motion? A little silicon spray on the bed of the machine may help it to slide more easily.

Make sure you have plenty of table space to the side and back of the machine to take the weight of the quilt. An ironing board can help here if it is set up at the side. An alternative is the new type of table you can buy with an insert to sit your machine into so that it is, essentially, a 'flat-bed' machine.

dia. 4. Some quilting ideas

a. Quilted 'in the ditch' around each patch

b. Quilted around each block and across diagonals

c. Quilted around each block and across diagonals with gentle curves

d. Quilted around each block, across the diagonals with straight and curved lines

e. Quilted around each block and then with interlocking circles

f. Quilted in the ditch and with curved lines in plain squares

g. Quilted in the ditch, with two main diagonals and with curved lines in some plain squares

h. Allover vermicelli quilting

Where to quilt dia. 4a -h

The most basic form of machine quilting is 'quilting in the ditch'. This is a straight line stitched in the seams of the patchwork. It is usually done with invisible (monofilament) or toning thread so it doesn't show.
Another basic form of quilting is to stitch ¼" away from the seam lines.
Spaces within blocks can be simply divided with straight or curved lines.

As with hand quilting, an all-over pattern can be stitched on the quilt top, disregarding the patchwork pattern. This is most often seen with basic longarm quilting designs.

Stitching

We are finally ready to go. Your machine is set up, the threads chosen and set up, the new needle in place, the quilt pinned, marked and ready.

Ideally you should start to quilt in the middle. This isn't always possible; the middle of one side may be an alternative if you are stitching from one side to another. Or, as with hand quilting, you can start in one corner. Whichever way you do it, be consistent and work gradually outwards so that any tendency for the fabric to creep means that it is creeping to unstitched areas where it won't form the dreaded pucker or tuck. Unless you are entering your quilt for a juried show don't fret about tucks and wrinkles on the back; they happen to all of us at one time or another.

11. Fold or roll the quilt under the machine arm

Roll or fold or pleat your quilt so that it fits under the arm of the machine, photo 11. You can hold these folds in place if you like with a few bicycle clips – you can also buy special quilters clips that are like bicycle clips with teeth. You may also need to support some of the quilt over your shoulder to stop it from dragging away from the needle at the front.

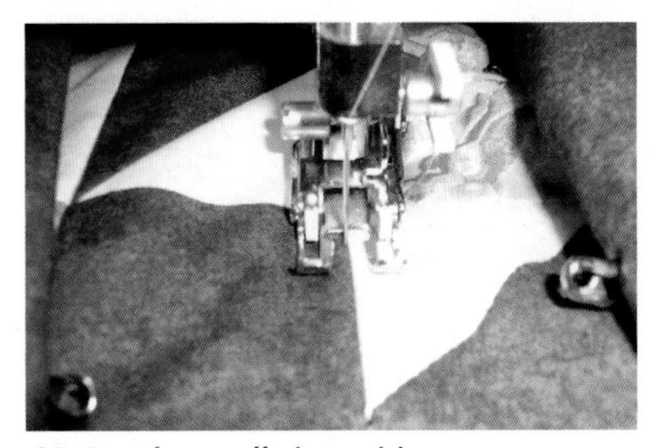

12. Put the needle in position

Once you and your quilt are in position and reasonably comfortable, take a deep breath... put the needle down in the place you want to start stitching, photo 12, hold the threads at the back so they don't get chewed up and dragged into the bowels of the machine, and do a few very small, almost on the spot, stitches to secure the threads. Now adjust the stitch length to the one you chose earlier and stitch to wherever you have decided this quilting line is going to finish – depending on your design you could do almost the entire quilt in the ditch by the time you run out of a 'continuous line'. To stop, reduce the stitch length back down to practically nothing for the last few stitches. Clip the threads, take the quilt out from under the machine and ... breathe. If you are making a wall hanging, just clip the dangling threads. If the quilt will be washed and handled a lot, it may be better to use a needle to take the top thread through to the back, knot the two together and run them into the wadding.

Additional quilting can be added in coloured, or invisible, thread to fill in any large spaces. Use straight lines or gentle flowing curves to create a border design that can be stitched using

> **TIP**
>
> *Keep a 'scribble sandwich' by your machine. Aim to do just ten minutes scribbling and doodling every day, and also every time you sit down to sew on another project. Within a very few weeks you could be stitching like a pro.*

the walking foot, photo 13. It is a good idea when changing direction, or pausing to move the quilt or your hands, while quilting to try to have the needle down in the fabric so it doesn't pull away from the line of stitch.

13. Straight lines and gentle curves make a border design

Free-motion quilting

At this point you may feel you want add a little more to your top – perhaps some squiggles and loops. It is time to tackle free-motion quilting, photo 14. Make yourself another practice piece first.

14. Free motion quilting example (by C. June Barnes)

To set the machine up you need to put the feed dogs down and use a darning foot. Check in your handbook how to do this for your particular machine. In free motion quilting the needle is static, you move the quilt. Play with your practice piece. Try to keep the motor running at an even speed to suit you and move the fabric round under the needle. The faster you move, the bigger the stitches; don't move at all and you end up with all your stitches in one place (and a big knot). Play around with different types of doodle to see which ones you find it easiest to do, dia 5.

dia. 5. Doodles

When you start free-motion quilting on your real quilt try to keep movements to a comfortable minimum in one area at a time as this is easier than manipulating a large sandwich through the machine.

Before you do it for real though, practice with pencil and paper to understand how it works and begin visualising what you can make happen. Hold the pencil still – or get someone else to – and you move the paper. Draw your design repeatedly, either with a pencil on paper or with your finger on the table until it becomes almost instinctive before you try to stitch it. Vermicelli is usually a good starting choice for a background filler but don't limit yourself, try other scribbly loops and swirls.

You can also draw designs onto tear-away tissue paper as before, but these can be more intricate for free motion. Again, don't forget – you are moving the fabric, you don't have to turn it to follow the lines just move it forwards, backwards and sideways.

For free-motion you need to be quite relaxed to get the timing right and the loops and swirls flowing – a glass of wine (or gin apparently) beforehand can work wonders! Do take a break every so often, though, to relax your shoulder and neck muscles. Being hunched over your machine, all tense in an effort to get it 'right' can play havoc. It is meant to be fun and enjoyable. Isn't it?!

Hand quilting

The advantage of hand quilting, like that of hand piecing, is that it can be very portable. Photo 15 shows the maximum equipment you are likely to need.

Do I need a hoop or frame? and if so, which one?

Hand quilting is a running stitch worked through three layers. That's it – nothing more – and just that simple. It is possible to achieve a smooth neat finish without using a hoop or frame and, contrary to the current laws of the Quilting Police, it is perfectly okay to quilt without any of the extra hardware, just holding the work in your hands. Most people feel that working without a hoop or frame feels easier and more natural, nearer to "ordinary" sewing. It can be a considerable leap and change of comfort level to using a hoop or frame. It's a leap that can be made but usually requires perseverance and a little patience. Don't feel that this is something that you must master first time around. Quilting is meant to be enjoyed so it's probably more important to just get on and stitch through the three layers to make some of that lovely touchy texture. Lots of quilters use a hoop. An embroidery hoop isn't sufficiently robust so you'll need a hoop specifically for quilting – a 14" diameter works well – but it doesn't have to be a fancy hoop on a stand to begin with. Lots of quilters use square clip frames. Like hoops these come in a variety of sizes and again we think a medium size somewhere between 14 and 17" is a good choice.

15. Hand quilting equipment

If you try out a hoop or clip frame you will come to the thorny question of tension – how taut should the work be? Is there a correct tension? Let's just say that everyone develops their own preferences over the course of time and we encourage you to experiment with various degrees of tension to find what suits you best. As a very general rule of thumb if the work is very tight or very slack it can be quite frustrating trying to get the needle back to the top.

Both hoops or clip frames can be used for full size quilts. Begin working at the centre and move the hoop or frame so that you work systematically out from the centre to the edges, or begin at one corner and work along to the opposing corner before returning to the original edge and working along again in the same direction.

Some quilters use a traditional frame – the wonderful bonus of these frames is that they are relatively quick to set up and the quilt layers do not require basting, the down side of these frames is that they require space.

Needles and thread

The traditional choice for quilting needles is the type known as betweens – we have always wondered what they were between but never found the answer! Betweens are short sturdy needles with a rounded eye and are available in mixed or single size packets. A good starting size might be a #9. Betweens are suited to the rock and roll stitching that usually goes with using a hoop or frame because the shorter length is easier to rock back and forth, longer needles such as sharps would probably work better for quilting in your hand.

16. Detail of hand quilting

Choose a good quality cotton thread for your quilting. General purpose sewing thread is likely to be a polyester blend which can stretch and has a tendency to fray. Try several different brands if you can and see what the differences are and what seems to suit you best.
Don't agonise too much over the precise matching of thread colour to fabric – often a dark neutral such as grey will look good on all the fabrics and, if you must match a little, aim for a thread which is slightly darker than the fabric, photo 16. Having the thread slightly darker seems to add depth to the stitched texture and can be very effective, photo 17.

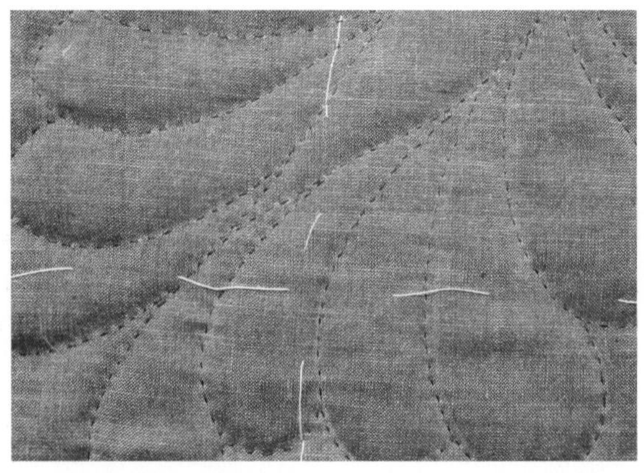

17. Using a darker thread

Thimbles

Do you really need one? Have you ever used one? It's very likely that at some point in your future hand quilting career you will feel that a thimble might be useful. Pushing a needle through three layers is so much easier if you have the protection of a thimble somewhere on your sewing hand. If you have never worn a thimble for any other sewing we think it's a good idea to change the habits of a lifetime and get used to wearing one. Whatever type of thimble you choose it should fit well without stopping your circulation. If you don't get along with rigid metal thimbles seek out some of the alternatives – leather, plastic, adhesive bandage wraps, adhesive "dots", surgical tape – the list is almost endless.

18. Quilting stitch

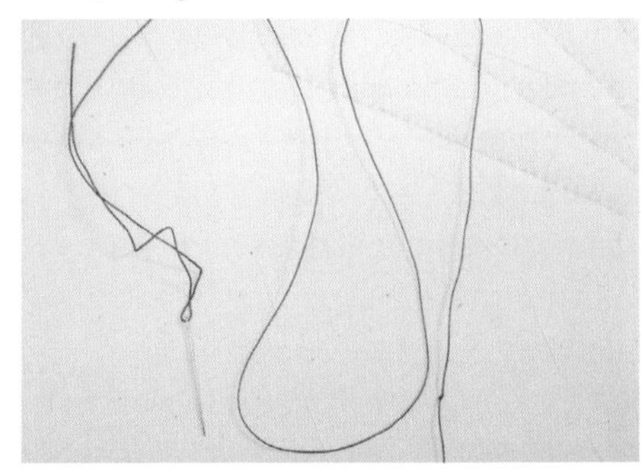

a. Ready to start, note the knot at the end

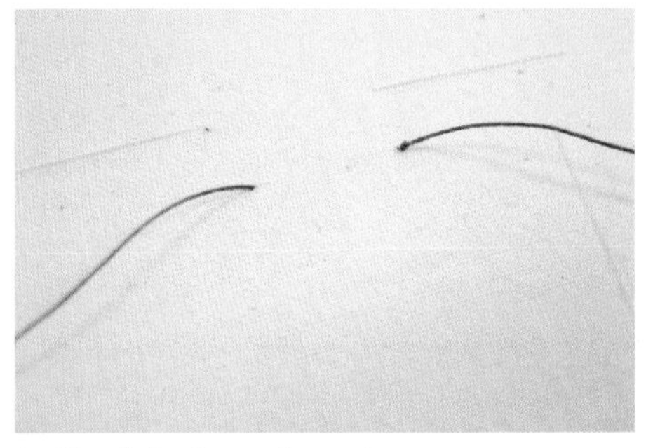

b. 'Pop' the knot through

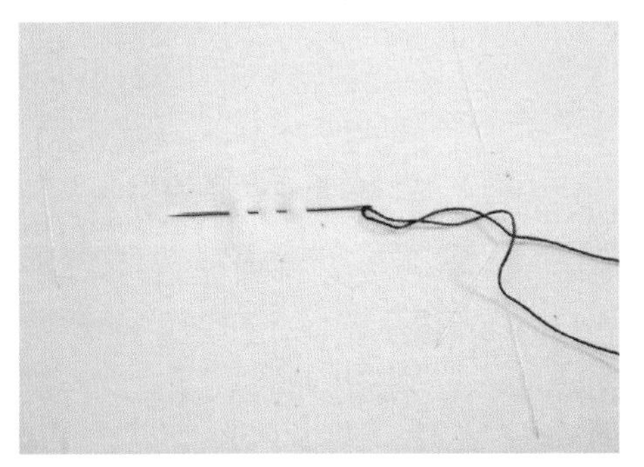

c. Several stitches on the needle

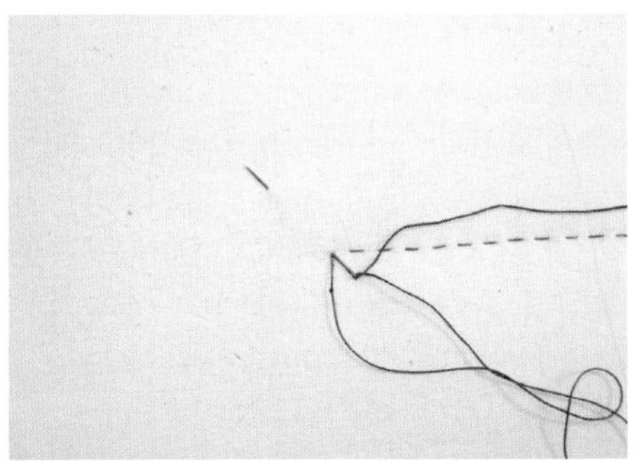

d. Finish off by making a small knot near the surface ...

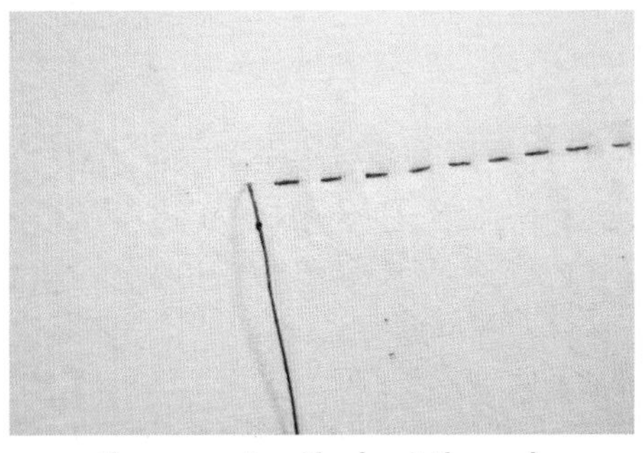

e. ... then popping the knot through the top fabric.

Start to finish

With quilting lines marked and the layers tacked together it's time to get down to the actual stitching. Thread your needle and cut a length of thread about 18inches. Knot the end leaving a short tail of thread beyond the knot, photo 18a. Quilting is begun, worked and finished on the top layer. Put the needle in through the top layer and slide it along the batting to bring it out to the top again where you want your line of quilting to begin. "Pop" the knot through the top fabric so that it lies in the batting just below the surface, photo 18b. Now you can make neat running stitches through the three layers following the line you have marked. Take one stitch at a time or, if you prefer, more than one. If you are working in your hand and not on a hoop or frame, loading several stitches on the needle is a practical possibility, photo 18c. If you are using a hoop or frame for the first time focus your thoughts on making just one stitch at a time to begin with. The traditional rocking technique depends on rocking the needle back and forth to make stitches and every quilter we've seen does this slightly differently, which leads us to conclude that there is no One Way to Quilt. We think it's a good idea to watch as many demonstrations as you can, look at lots of books and magazines and take classes as available.

Finishing off your thread is broadly the reverse of the starting procedure – take your last complete stitch and bring your needle to the top as if you were going to continue. Slide a knot down the thread so that it is near to the surface of the work. Put the needle back into the exit hole and slide it away along the batting before bringing the needle back through the top fabric a short distance away, photo 18d. Pull the needle through so that the knot "pops" through the fabric and buries itself in the batting, photo 18e. Hold the thread taut and clip it, then do the same with the tail of thread at the start.

Hand quilting is not the fastest process – it does take time, but so many quilters enjoy the process and find it very therapeutic. It really isn't anything to get anxious about, improvement comes from doing it not thinking about it. Just do it, relax and enjoy the texture you are creating.

Over the years Barbara has developed a **Little List of Don'ts:**

- **Don't** look at the back of your work – it will only make you anxious
- **Don't** unpick lots of stitches – it will only slow your progress
- **Don't** be too critical – everything improves with time
- **Don't** sit hunched over your quilting for more than half an hour at a time – it will only make you stiff
- **Don't** make do with general lighting – a good worklamp is a must and so much better for your eyesight

19. Quilting in progress – note the tacking

This has been a very brief overview of quilting. For further information and designs have a look at the many books available on the subject. We hesitate to recommend any particular one as there are so many and they are each good in their own way – you need to find the book that 'speaks' to you. But the best way to learn is to go to a class, there are plenty around the country – find one near you and go. You can read a book and follow the pictures but nothing beats hands-on experience with an expert at your shoulder guiding you through step by step and helping you to find a solution to your problems.

Finishing the Quilt

Bindings, labels and sleeves

Binding

"Bind to finish" – three little words which can spread almost as much dismay as that other overused and famous phrase "quilt as desired". Binding is not difficult and can make a huge difference to the overall look of a quilt so we think it's worth taking the time to do it well. There is more than one binding technique, indeed whole books have been written on the subject, but we're going to feature the double fold binding that we use most often.

Preparing the fabric is an important step – as we saw with machine piecing a little spray starch can work wonders and makes measuring and cutting fabric so much easier. So we're going to recommend that you spray starch and press the fabric you plan on using for the binding.

For a regular square or rectangular quilt you can cut binding strips on the straight grain, for a scalloped edge it will be easier to work with binding strips cut on the crossgrain. We mostly use straight grain strips for our bindings. The width of the strips is determined by the width you want the finished binding to be when viewed from the top side of the quilt – let's say that measurement is ½". For double fold binding you multiply this by 4 so that makes 2". Now we add on ½" for the seam allowances which makes 2½". This is the width of the binding strip. The length of each strip very much depends on the fabric available but it's really helpful if you can cut from a full (42" – 44") width of fabric. Here's yet another use for those lovely Jelly Roll strips!

You'll almost certainly have to join several strips together to make sufficient length of binding – join strips with right sides together at 90°, photo 1a, mark and stitch on the diagonal, photo1b, then trim, photo1c, and press the seam open.

1. Joining binding strips

a. Mark 45° line

b. Stitch

c. Cut

Check that you have joined sufficient strips together before going any further – the traditional checking procedure we both use is to lay the miles of strip along all four sides of the quilt and then add in a hefty measure of insurance. Well-organised quilters probably measure all four sides of the quilt and add them together and then add on a further 10" to allow for joining and corners. There is absolutely nothing worse than finding that the binding is 2" too short, so we tend to err on the side of generosity and would probably add in a full length strip and be prepared to cut away and 'waste' binding.

Once you have a strip of the required length and width it's time to approach the ironing board and carefully press the strip in half along the length. Take care to press rather than iron – you'll remember that ironing can distort fabric, so resist the urge to sweep the iron around.

It's not always possible to prepare and attach the binding in the same session – if you need to store the freshly pressed binding, rolling it around a piece of card, an empty bottle or looping it on a clothes airer or hanger are all good options for temporary storage.

Prepare the quilt

Immediately before binding is a good time to give your quilt a thorough going over, clipping away stray threads and making sure all four sides are trimmed to crisp straight edges that have appropriate and matching measurements. Then you're ready to start pinning the binding strip into position with raw edges matched to the edges of the quilt and the fold of the binding to the middle of the quilt. Where you begin pinning very much depends on which corner strategy you select – see below – but whichever you choose, fine flat headed pins are perfect for the job. Pin at right angles to the outside edge at intervals of approximately 3", photo 2.

2. Pin at right angles

Corners, corners

There are two ways of dealing with the corner situation. Method One is to use butted binding and Method Two is to make a mitred binding. Years ago we thought butted binding was the easiest and therefore the best and so we both bound lots of quilts this way. More recently we've conquered our fear of mitred binding and found that its not at all hard to do, in fact now Barbara is convinced that it's the easier option. We'll describe both methods for you – why not try both of them out on an unwanted block so you can see how they work?

Butted corners

- Pin two opposing sets of binding and stitch into place. We favour pinning and stitching binding to the longer sides first followed by the shorter top and bottom edges, photo 3a.
- Use a walking or even feed foot on your machine and consider lengthening the stitch setting just a fraction. Stitch with the usual ¼" seam allowance from top edge to bottom edge.
- Trim threads and the binding strip so that it is level with the remaining unbound edges of the quilt. Fold the binding over to the back of the quilt and pin in position, photo 3b.

3. Butted corners

a. Pin to long edges

b. Fold to back

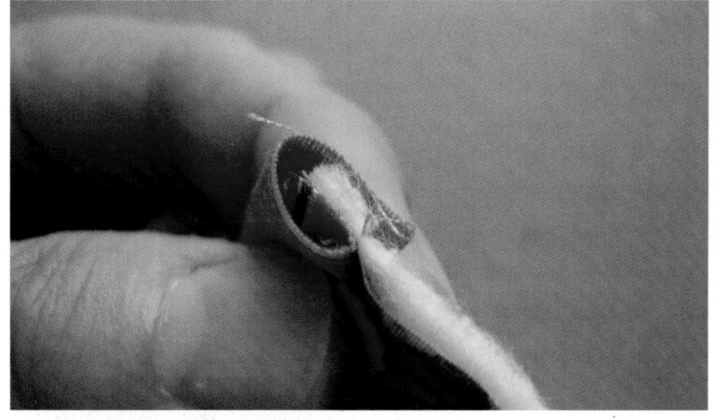

c. Binding not 'filled' with quilt

d. Leave 'turn in' allowance at each end

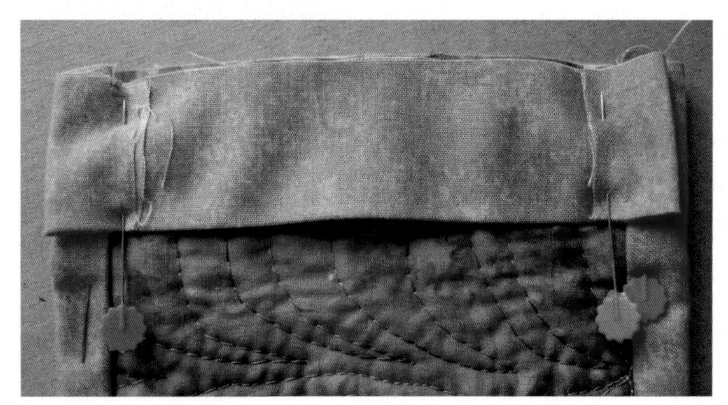

e. Fold in line with quilt edge

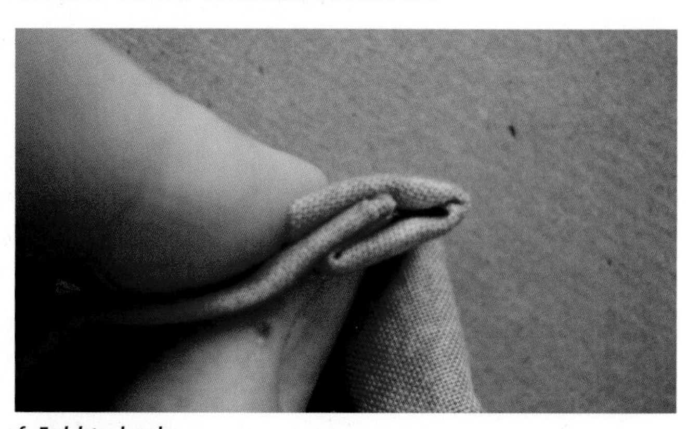

f. Fold to back

Note that binding looks best if it is 'filled' with quilt – you can see in the pictures that our sample quilt does not extend fully into the binding which will make an unsatisfactory finish, photo 3c.

- Position and pin the second set of binding strips along the remaining unbound edges. Leave a short 'turn in' allowance at the start and finish of each strip, photo 3d, then turn in so folded edge of this allowance is in line with the folded edge of the first turned back binding, photo 3e.
- Stitch the strips in place, beginning and finishing just a little way short of the outside edge.
- Fold all binding strips over to the back of the quilt and pin in place, photo 3f. Hemstitch to finish using a small neat stitch and thread which tones with the binding. Oversew at the corners using a matching thread and neat stitches – contrasting thread was used in photo 3g for better visibility.

g. Oversew ends (normally a matching thread would be used!)

Mitred corners

- Begin pinning the folded binding strip in place about two thirds of the way down one of the longer sides, photo 4a. Pin to the first corner then stitch to a marked point which is ¼" in from both edges, photo 4b. One trick that we picked up from master piecers Harriet Hargrave and Christine Porter is to stop stitching exactly on the point and stitch off at 45° – this helps to keep the mitred corner flat, photo 4c.
- Cut the threads and pull the quilt away from the machine so that you can fold the binding away from the quilt, photo 4d. Keep the edges of the binding level with the quilt edges and use a pin to hold the 45° fold in place, photo 4e.
- Refold the binding back over the pin, photo 4f, then fold down as shown, photo 4g. Mark ¼", photo 4h, and pin to the next corner before stitching.
- Continue in this way until you have completed all four corners.

4. Mitred corners

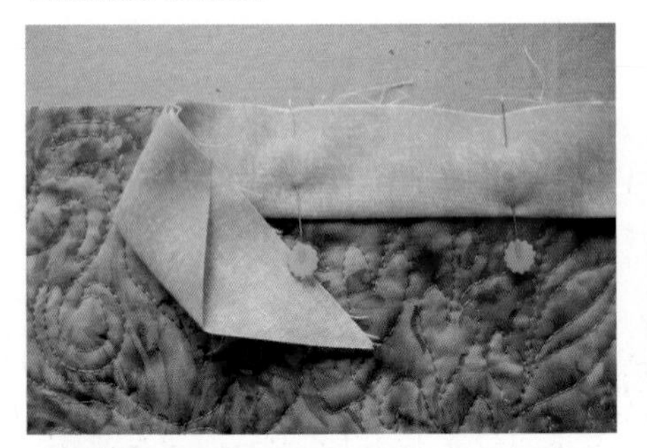

a. Pin starting ⅔ down side

b. Mark ¼" from end

c. Stitch off at 45°

d. First fold

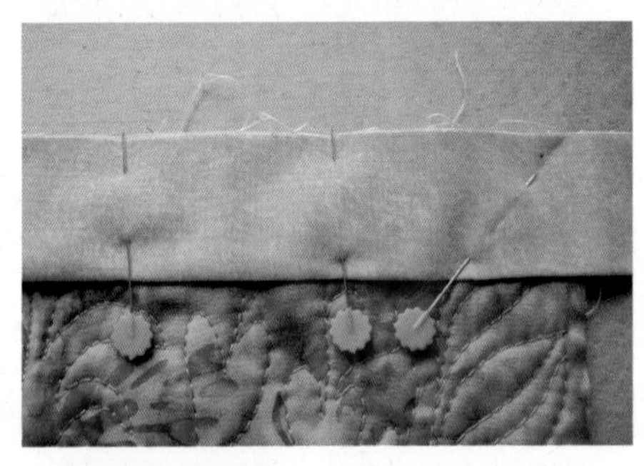

e. Pin along fold

f. Refold against pin

g. Second fold

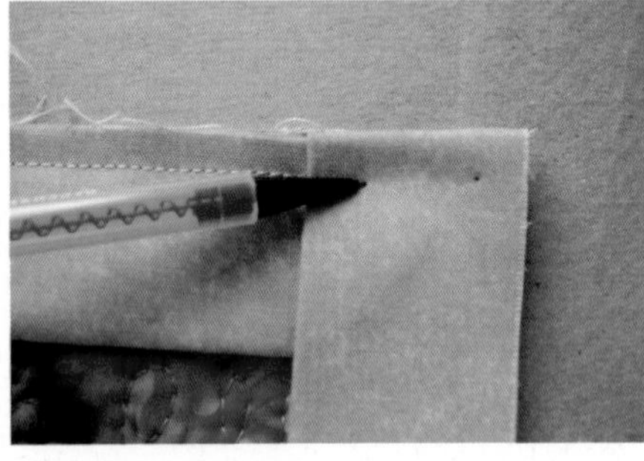

h. Pin to next corner, then stitch

Adding the binding

Our favourite joining method for binding is one we learned from US quilter and teacher Sherri Bain Driver and, like everything else, it's easy to do if you concentrate and work slowly and carefully through the steps.

You need to have a 45° angled edge to the beginning of your binding strip.

- Leave about 12" of unbound manoeuvring space between the start and finish of your stitching. Cut threads and remove the quilt from the machine to a flat surface, photo 5a.
- Open out the end tail of the binding and pin it to the quilt edge. Open out the beginning tail of binding and lay this over the pinned ending tail, photo 5b.
- Draw a line on the WS of the ending tail that matches the angle of the beginning tail (i.e. 45°) – check that both angles are 45° and following the same direction, photo 5c.
- Draw a second line on the WS of the ending tail ½" away from the first line, photo 5d. This is a cutting line. Cut on this line, photo 5e.
- Now fold the quilt so that you can put RS of the binding strips together, offsetting the points slightly so that the strips will match ¼" in from the edge, photo 5f. Stitch with a ¼" seam and press this seam open, photo 5g.
- Press the joined binding back into half, photo 5h, and finish stitching the binding to the quilt, photo 5i.
- Turn the binding over to the back of the quilt, photo 5j, and stitch into place by hand, making sure that the binding covers the line of machine stitch. You may want to carefully trim away excess backing and wadding at the corners. The folds turn over into place on the front, photo 5k, and back, photo 5l, with a mitre on both sides.

5. Joining mitred binding

a. Leave manoeuvring space

b. Overlap end

c. Draw first line

d. Draw second line

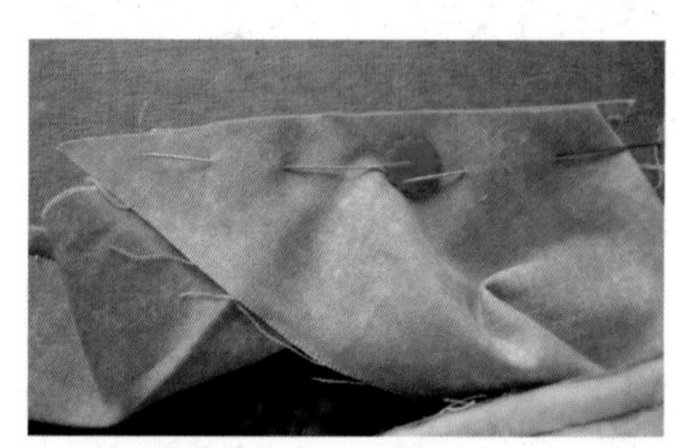

e. RS binding strips together, points offset

f. Press seams open

g. Fold in half

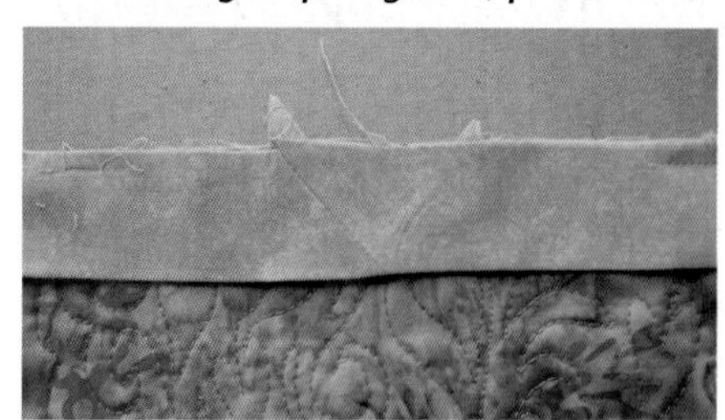

h. Complete stitching to quilt

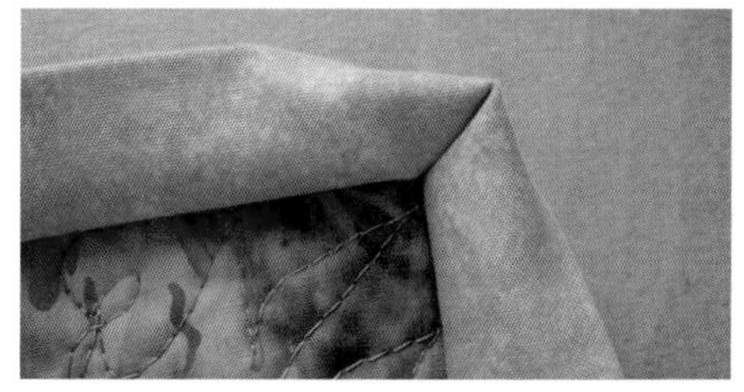

i. Turn binding to back of quilt

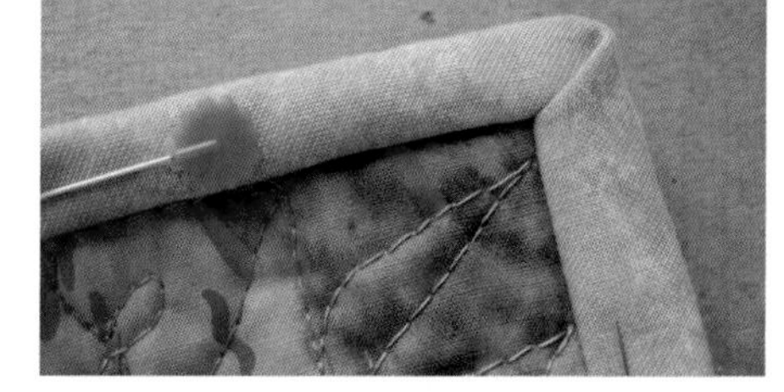

j. Corner viewed from RS

k. Corner viewed from back

How to make your own continuous bias binding

This is useful for binding quilts with rounded corners or scalloped edges.

- Cut a square of your binding fabric, dia. 1a. The table in the Quick Reference will tell you how big a square you need.
- Cut the square in half diagonally, dia. 1b.
- Sew the triangles together, dia. 2a – d.

dia. 1. Binding

a. cut a square

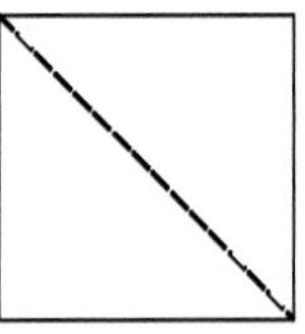

b. cut in half

dia. 2. Resew triangles together

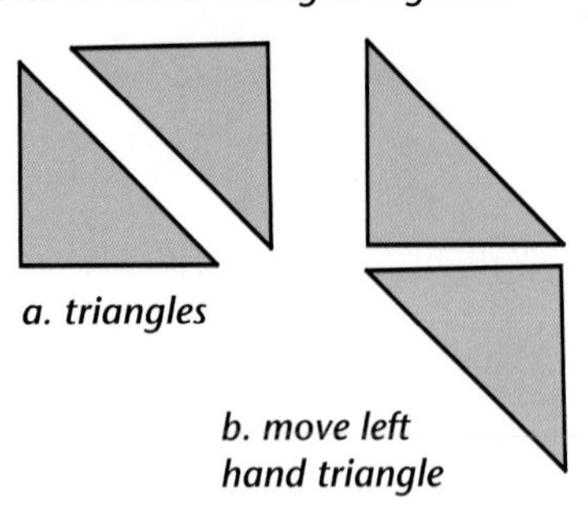

a. triangles

b. move left hand triangle

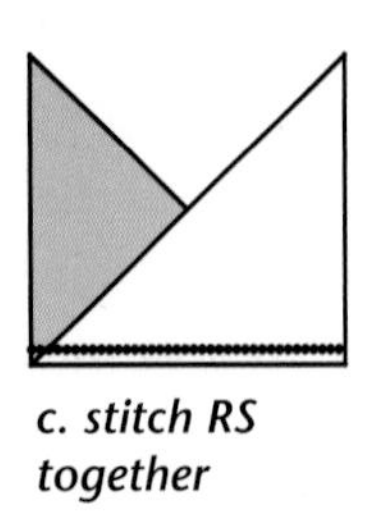

c. stitch RS together

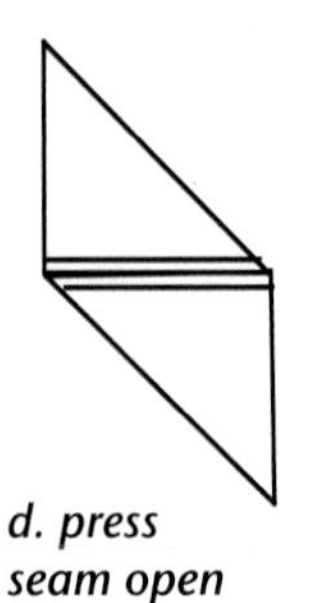

d. press seam open

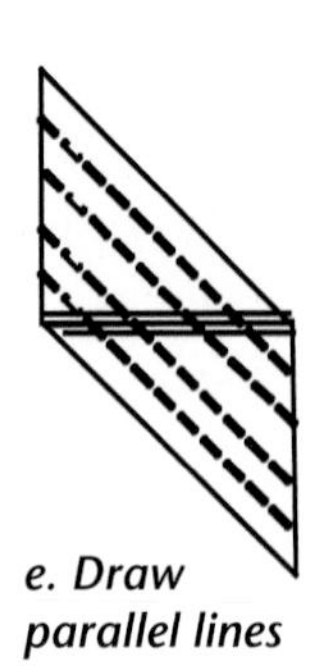

e. Draw parallel lines

- Draw lines parallel to the longer sides (2½" apart for double bindings), dia. 2e.
- Fold into tube putting shorter edges right sides together and off-setting the drawn lines by one.
- Stitch along this short edge.
- Cut along drawn line(s).

All you have to do now is fold it, press it and use it!

There are lots of different ways of tackling binding, none of them difficult – we've only described two for you to try. Look out for the many books on the subject and remember that there is no substitute for actually doing it! Barbara found that her binding skills were greatly improved by working her way through 25 quilts of different sizes for a book deadline!

Labels and sleeves

Labels and hanging sleeves provide the final finishing touches to say who made the quilt and when, and to hang your wall-hanging or to display your quilt at a show.

Labels

A label at its simplest is just what it says – a label with your name and the date on. Depending on what you feel is appropriate there is much more information that can be included. The title of the quilt, inspiration source, materials and techniques used, your name, date started, date finished, name of the recipient and the occasion – birthday, wedding, anniversary etc. And please label all your work – it's not boastful or saying your work is wonderful, but labelling adds so much to each quilt's identity for years to come.

Making a label

The easiest way is just to write on the back of the quilt with a fabric marker pen (that doesn't wash out!). Alternatively you can write the details onto a piece of fabric and stitch it to the back of the quilt. Or you can get labels made for you – just like school name tapes.

You can use your machine to embroider the details – either free machine or using the decorative letters that some machines enable you to stitch. Or you can hand embroider …

Nowadays it is easy to buy (or prepare) printable fabric to feed through aninkjet printer. You could design yourself a whole sheet of labels using the "envelopes and labels" menu and print them off ready to attach to the back of your quilts. Don't go mad and print a couple of dozen with the same year on – unless you know you will make that many in a year. You may prefer to design and print one label at a time – any size up to A4 – as the need arises.

6. Labels

a. Written directly onto quilt back

b. Written and stitched, pinked edge

c. Hand stitched on front of quilt

d. Free machine stitched and appliquéd

e. Machine embroidered and appliquéd

f. Simple computer generated

h. Computer generated label with embroidery

dia. 4. Album block as a label

You can make mini-blocks with the left-overs to use as labels. Either the same block as on the front or you can make an Album block, dia. 4, with a space for your details designed in. The advantage of Album blocks is that they can sometimes be incorporated in the front of the quilt as well as used on the back.

You may have a block that didn't quite work out or get included in the quilt – this could be perfect to use as a label or part of a label.

Attaching a label

You can hem the fabric, or cut it with pinking shears. Tack it on leaving a raw edge or hem it neatly turning under the raw edges. The choice is yours. If you get ahead of yourself you can attach the label at the same time as the binding and stitch the label firmly in place in a corner as you bind the quilt, leaving you with only two sides to hem down.

Sleeves

If you just intend to hang your quilt at home and never exhibit it then you can make the sleeve of a width to suit your hanging arrangements. However, if you intend entering the quilt for a show then do read the hanging instructions carefully and ensure the sleeve meets their criteria – usually 4" deep.

A temporary sleeve can be made from calico or something similar. A permanent sleeve should (if possible) be the same fabric as the backing – but you may prefer a contrast, or a pieced sleeve to match the front.

Making a sleeve

Cut a strip of fabric twice the finished width of the sleeve plus a seam allowance. You may have to join strips if you are putting a sleeve on a bed quilt.
Fold under the short ends twice and stitch to form a hem.
Fold the sleeve in half lengthways and stitch along the long raw edge.
Turn right side out – you should now have a long tube.
Press it so the seam is in the middle of the back. This gives a folded edge to the long sides of the sleeve and makes attaching the sleeve easier.

Attaching a sleeve

There are several methods available to attach the sleeve.
If it is a temporary sleeve for a show then just stitch it down with straight running stitches close to the edges – but don't forget to leave the ends open! Also take care that your stitches don't show through to the front of the quilt. (Ask us how we know both these things!)

An easy, more permanent method is to catch the top edge of the sleeve in with the binding then hem the sides and bottom edge by hand.
Alternatively just hem the whole sleeve in place – if you are confident with your machine you could use the blind hemming option – or hand stitch.

A sleeve can go the whole width of the back of the quilt, or can be in sections, leaving gaps – again it depends on how you prefer to hang your quilts, or on instructions for the show organisers – for UK exhibitions the hanging sleeve is usually (finished) 4inches deep.

Some quilters solve the "label and sleeve" issue by combining the two which makes a lot of sense, particularly if your quilt will be hung in a show or on a wall at home. Make your label and stitch it to the sleeve fabric so that it will face out when the sleeve is in position. It's almost too easy!

dia. 5. Sleeves

a. Continous sleeve

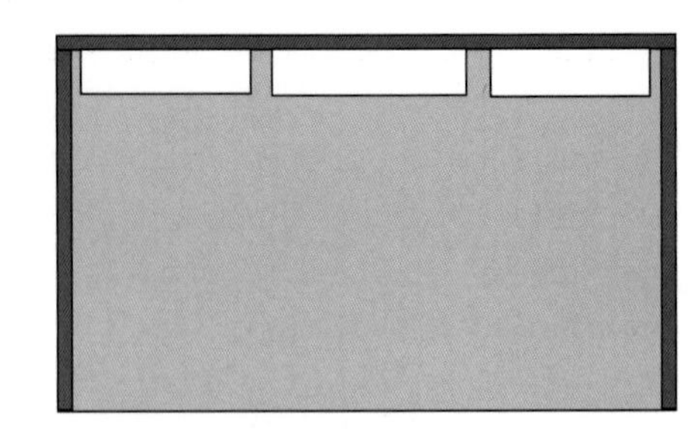

b. Sleeve in sections

Project – Sawtooth Star

A simple wallhanging or lap quilt

Quilt size: 36" square
Block size: 8"

Requirements

- 1m fabric A (blue)
- 1m fabric B (marbled)
- 0.5m fabric C (yellow)
- 1m wadding
- 1m backing

Cutting

From A cut:
5, 4½" squares
16, 2½" squares
4, 5¼" squares cut in 4 diagonally
4, 6½" wide strips for borders

From B cut:
20, 2½" squares
4, 4½" squares
4 2½" wide strips for binding

From C cut:
20, 2½" x 4½" rectangles
16, 2⅞" squares cut in 2 diagonally

Stretched 9-Patch Blocks

- Stitch 2½" B squares to either end of half 2½ x 4½" C rectangles, dia.1.
- Stitch remaining C rectangles to either side A 4½" squares, dia.2.
- Stitch rows together to complete block, dia.3.

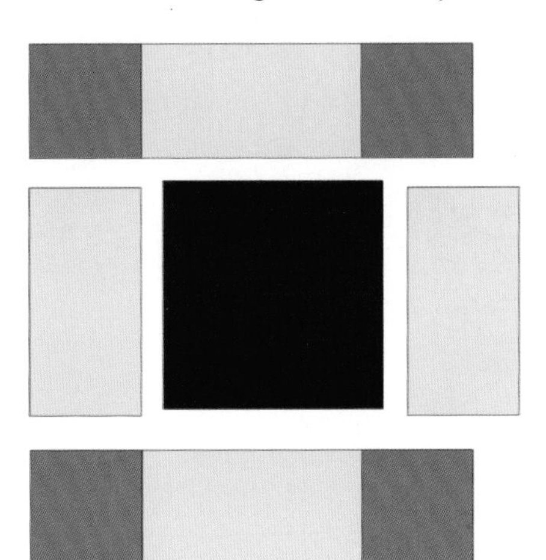

dia.1 Stitch small squares to rectangles

dia. 2. Stitch centre square to rectangles

dia. 3 complete block

Sawtooth Star

- Stitch C triangles to either side A triangles, dia.4.
- Stitch A 2½" squares to each end half of units from Step 1, dia.5.
- Stitch remaining Step 1 units to either side B 4½" squares, dia.6.
- Stitch rows together to complete block, dia.7.

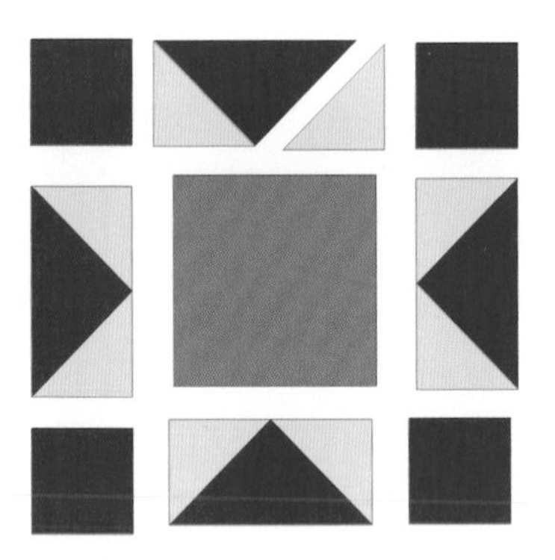

dia. 4. Stitch triangles

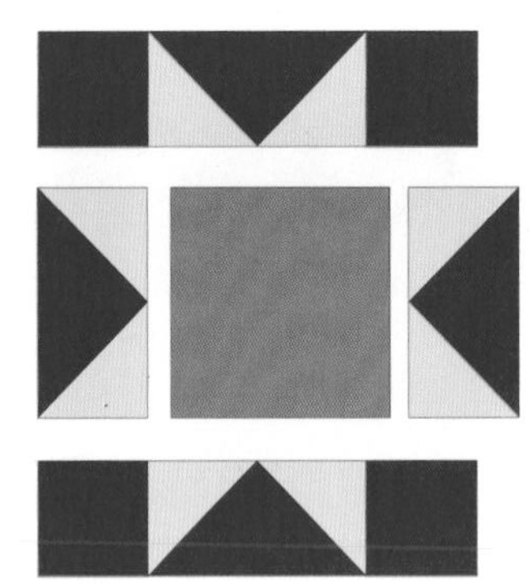

dia. 5. Stitch small squares to triangle units

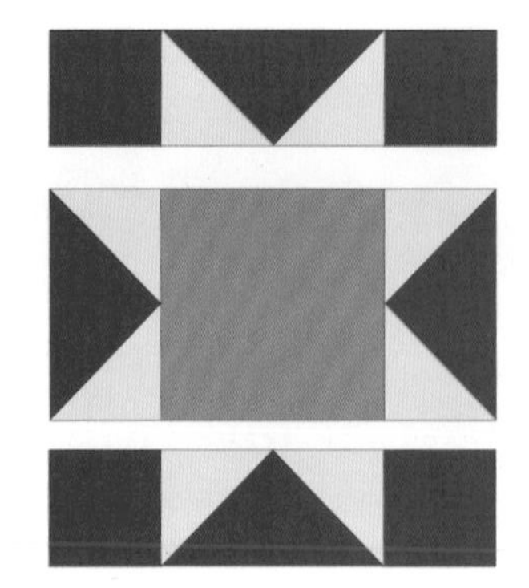

dia. 6. Stitch centre square to triangle units

dia. 7. Complete block

Quilt top

- Lay blocks out as shown, dia.8.
- Stitch into rows.
- Stitch rows together to complete, dia.9.

dia. 8. Lay blocks out and stitch into rows

dia. 9. Complete quilt top

Border

- Measure quilt width across middle
- Cut 2 A strips this length.
- Stitch to top and bottom of quilt.
- Measure quilt length down centre.
- Cut 2 A strips this length.
- Stitch to sides of quilt.

Completion

- Make quilt sandwich
- Quilt as desired.
- Bind using B strips for double-fold binding.
- Add a label and hanging sleeve to complete.

You could make this simple quilt in a number of different colourways. Here are a few examples, dia.10. See how changing the emphasis of light and dark can alter the whole appearance of the quilt top.

dia. 10. Different colourways

Quick reference

Need a quick reminder of seam allowances and measurements? – you should find most of them here.

Squares and rectangles

Add ½" to the finished unit size – e.g. for a finished size 2" square, cut a 2½" square.

Half–square triangles

Add ⅞" to the finished unit size. Cut squares to this measurement and cut in half diagonally.

Finished size of square (inches)	Size of square to cut (inches)
2	2⅞
2½	3⅜
3	3⅞
3½	4⅜
4	4⅞
4½	5⅜

Quarter–square triangles

Add 1¼" to the finished unit size. Cut squares to this measurement and cut in 4 diagonally.

Finished size of square (inches)	Size of square to cut (inches)
2	3¼
2½	3¾
3	4¼
3½	4¾
4	5¼
4½	5¾

Half-rectangles (Long triangles)

These are made by cutting a rectangle in half to give two identical triangles. Cut a rectangle 2⅝" wider than the short side of the triangle and 1¼" longer than the long side. For a 2 x 4" triangle cut a 2⅝" x 5¼" rectangle. To cut mirror image triangles cut another rectangle across the opposite diagonal.

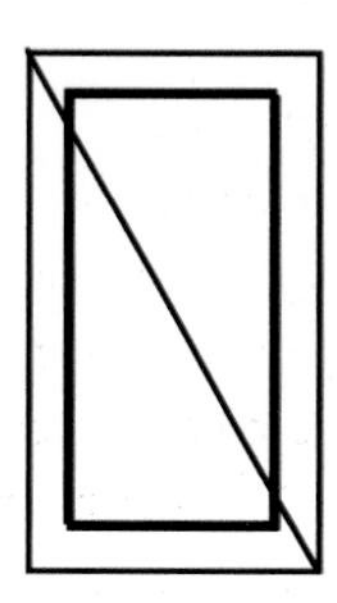

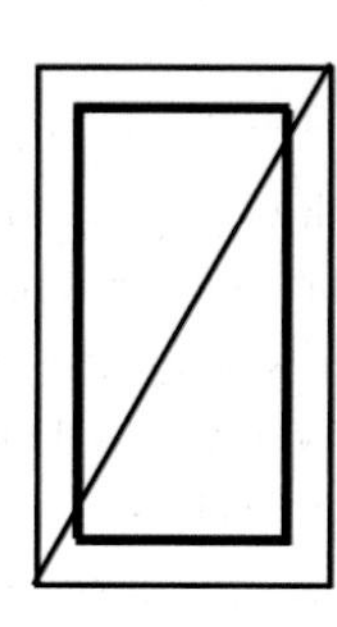

Isosceles triangle

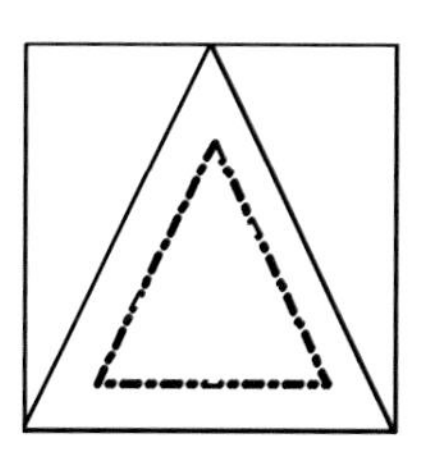

This is the one which, combined with a pair of long triangles, makes up a square. Cut a square 1" larger all round than the finished size – for a 2" triangle, cut a 3" square. Mark the midpoint of the top of the square – this is the triangle apex.

Equilateral (60°) triangle

Cut a strip ¾" wider than the required height of the triangle and add ⅞" to the finished length.

Diamonds

30° Cut a strip ½" wider than height of diamond, Add 1" to finished length.
45° Cut a strip ½" wider than height of diamond. Add ¾" to finished length.
60° Cut a strip ½" wider than the height of diamond, add ⅝" to finished length.

Magic formula for setting triangles for quilts set on point

The magic number to remember is 1.414.
For edge (or side) triangles (quarter-square triangles) - multiply by 1.414 and add 1¼" seam allowance e.g. finished block size of 8": 8 x 1.414 = 11.312 + 1.25 (seam allowance) = 12.562; round up to the nearest ⅛. = 12⅝".
For corner triangles (half-square triangles) divide by 1.414 and add ⅞"
e.g. finished block size of 8": 8 ./. 1.414 + 0.875 (⅞) = 6.5327 rounded up = 6⅝"

Continuous bias binding

To make continuous bias, you start with a square.

Size of square (inches)	Length of binding (yards)
8	0.7
9	0.9
10	1
11	1.3
12	1.6
14	2.1
16	2.8
18	3.6
20	4.4
25	6.9
36	14.4

Yardage calculations

Fabric used for patchwork is generally 44" wide (112cm). Check how wide the fabric is before you buy, because if it is less than 44" you will probably need to buy more than indicated in the tables. Always buy a little extra to allow for shrinkage and for the fabric being cut off the grain.

We have assumed that the easiest way to cut shapes from the fabric is to cut strips and slice the strips into the required shapes. This is fine for rotary cutting, if you prefer to draw round templates and then cut out with scissors you may have a little more wastage and should allow for this in your shopping list. For all shapes, to calculate the amount of fabric you need, work out how many of that shape will fit (with seam allowance included) across the width of the fabric. Then work out how wide a strip you will need for the width of the shape. Calculate how many strips you need for the number of shapes to cut and multiply this by the width of the strips to give you the yardage.

Squares

Add ½" seam allowance (¼" all round).
The number of squares that can be cut:

cut size	finished size	from a fat quarter	from ½ yd	from ¾ yd	1yd
1½"	1"	168	348	522	696
2"	1½"	99	198	286	396
2½"	2"	56	119	170	238
3"	2½"	42	84	126	168
3½"	3"	30	60	84	120
4"	3½"	20	44	66	99
4½"	4"	16	36	54	72
5"	4½"	16	24	40	56
5½"	5"	9	21	28	42
6"	5½"	9	21	28	35
6½"	6"	9	12	24	30

Half-square triangles

To calculate the seam allowance, and thus the width of strip, or size of square, to cut you should add ⅞" to the finished size of the triangle.
The number of half square triangles that can be cut:

cut size	finished size	from a fat quarter	from ½ yd	from ¾ yd	1yd
1⅞"	1"	108	396	572	792
2⅜"	1½"	98	238	340	476
2⅞"	2"	72	168	252	336
3⅜"	2½"	50	120	168	240
3⅞"	3"	32	88	132	198
4⅜"	3½"	32	72	108	144
4⅞"	4"	18	48	80	112
5⅜"	4½"	18	48	64	96
5⅞"	5"	18	42	56	84
6⅜"	5½"	18	24	48	60
6 6/8"	6"	18	24	36	60

Quarter-square triangles

To calculate the seam allowance and thus the width of strip or size of square to cut you need to add 1¼" to the finished size of the triangle.
The number of quarter square triangles that can be cut:

cut size	finished size	from a fat quarter	from ½ yd	from ¾ yd	1yd
2¼"	1"	324	608	836	1140
2¾"	1½"	168	384	576	832
3¼"	2"	120	260	416	572
3¾"	2½"	80	176	308	396
4¼"	3"	80	160	240	320
4¾"	3½"	48	108	180	252
5¼"	4"	48	96	160	192
5¾"	4½"	36	84	112	168
6¼"	5"	24	56	112	140
6¾"	5½"	24	48	72	120
7¼"	6"	24	48	72	96

Diamonds

The diamonds used in eight-pointed stars are 45° diamonds. They can be cut from strips of fabric – measure the width of the diamond and add the seam allowance (¼") to both sides to give the width of strip to cut. Measure the length of the diamond and add ¾" to this measurement for the length of diamond to cut and to work out how many will fit across the width of the fabric.
The number of 45° diamonds that can be cut:

block size	from a fat quarter	from ½ yd	from ¾ yd	1yd
4"	108	216	329	432
6"	60	130	195	260
8"	40	88	132	176
9"	32	77	110	154
10"	28	70	100	140
12"	24	54	81	108

Craft away with our exciting range of books

Appliqué - A Cushion a Week

by Greta Fitchett

A book of new design projects, each exploring a different technique of appliqué.
Inside is a wealth of cushions to suit all from beginner to more advanced, ranging in size and shape.

Ref: APP

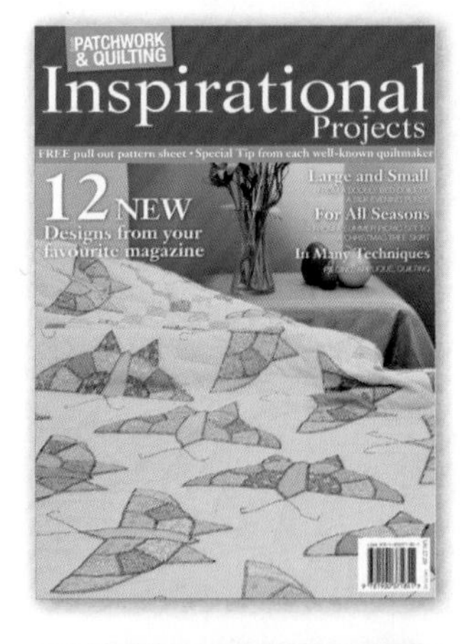

British Patchwork & Quilting Inspirational Projects

A special issue featuring 12 new designs from your favourite patchwork & quilting magazine.

Ref: PQSP10

Quilting with a Difference

by Nikki Tinkler

Learn how to add visual interest to the surface of your work while you quilt with award winning quilter, Nikki Tinkler.

Ref: QWAD

Two by Two

by Lesley Brankin

A complete pattern booklet.
Enjoy creating a truely time-less heirloom quilt that will be adored by children of all ages and loved by generation after generation.

Ref: TBT

Log Cabin Landscapes

by Dorothy Stapleton

Discover easy ways to stitch your own fabric houses, countrysides and scenes from around the world in this fantastic book for quilting enthusiasts.

Ref: LCL

Down on the Farm

by Lesley Brankin

A complete pattern booklet.
New foundation piecing pattern booklet available for this endearing lap sized quilt based on the childrens song 'Old MacDonald had a Farm'.

Ref: DOF

Stained Glass Patchwork for Christmas

by Gail Lawther

Create spectacular stained glass patchwork designs for the festive season with this fantastic book by award-winning quilter, Gail Lawther.

Ref: SGP

Indian Inspirations

by Gisela Thwaites

Discover how to enhance your own patchwork and quilting in this Indian-inspired resource for crazy patchwork enthusiasts of all skill levels.

Ref: IND

To order phone our hotline now! **UK:** 01684 588599

USA: 217 355 2970 **AUS:** (02) 9520 0933 **OTHERS:** +44 (0)1684 588599

Or shop online at www.trapletshop.com

Craft away with our exciting range of DVDs

Colour for Quilters

with Christine Porter

Join internationally renowned quilter Christine Porter as she leads you through the steps to great colour choices and beautiful quilts.

Ref: DV713

Also available on Blu-Ray

Ref: DV713HD

Borders, Bindings & Finishing Touches

with Christine Porter

In this DVD Christine demonstrates simple and effective techniques for choosing the border fabric, ideas for pieced borders and attaching the border accurately.

Ref: DV712

From Fabric to Quilt

with Christine Porter

This is Christine's guide for those who have ever marvelled at the creativity and artistry of the top quilters, and want to know how to go about designing and producing their own beautiful and original quilts.

Ref: DV710

Let's Get Started - Basic Patchwork Techniques

with Christine Porter

Join Christine Porter, as she guides you step by step through the essential techniques for creating fabulous patchwork.

Ref: DV704

Log Cabin Landscapes

with Dorothy Stapleton

Explore the world of the log cabin technique in this fantastic video by Dorothy Stapleton, which accompanies her book of the same name.

Ref: DV709

Stained Glass Patchwork 1 – Basic

with Gail Lawther

Take the mystery out of stained glass patchwork with this fantastic DVD by Gail Lawther, detailing easy ways of doing this very quick and dramatic technique.

Ref: DV705

Stained Glass Patchwork for Christmas

by Gail Lawther

Create spectacular stained glass patchwork designs for the festive season with this fantastic book by award-winning quilter, Gail Lawther.

Ref: SGP

Stained Glass Patchwork 2 – Advanced

with Gail Lawther

Discover many ways to vary, embellish and develop the basics of the stained glass patchwork technique to create your own unique quilts.

Ref: DV706

Sign up to our email newsletter at www.traplet.com/offers and get news on all our latest products and special offers – straight to your inbox!